ShagMail.com presents...

Great Sexpectations

Insight and wisdom for all your sexual queries.

Very special thanks to...

This book could not have been written without the support and encouragement from the many subscribers who have offered their suggestions, questions, and continual guidance. I would also like to thank my core of wonderful friends who never cease to expand my horizons and who selflessly offer themselves up as sacrificial lambs!

As we forge through the sexual frontier together, I must also thank everyone for tackling a sometimes sensitive subject with the most important attribute of all--humor! If we cannot laugh at ourselves, we would surely die of boredom.

Lastly, I have to acknowledge the powers that be at Shagmail and thank them for allowing me the opportunity to share my two cents about human sexuality and all of its mysteries. So far it's been quite a ride!

* * * **Table of Contents** * * *

An introduction by the *Great Sexpectations* author, Carmen,

When the powers that be at Shagmail first approached me to write a sex column, I had some serious reservations that provoked a great deal of reflection. After that heartfelt ten seconds had passed, they had their new sex writer. It was an opportunity to blaze a new trail, and with all of the sightseeing we can enjoy along the information superhighway, it was my one chance to offer something substantial. I felt that there was a legitimate need for a web publication that provided a healthy forum for real people with real issues. And so "Great Sexpectations" was born.

The mission was a simple one: write about helpful sexual information that many would not otherwise have the opportunity or the initiative to approach. Correct me if I'm wrong, but aren't there more than enough porn sites to satiate the masses and their never-ending quest for flesh? It is a rhetorical question, but the point is to provide something a little less crude and more casual in terms of human interest.

The mission worked, because most of my newsletter subscribers have shown themselves in earnest. They took the gloves off, said what they thought about the column, and offered their unbridled opinions about absolutely everything. The subscribers are indeed the lifeblood of the column, which is why I print their e-mail every week in a "Reader Comments" section.

I must admit the one thing I wasn't prepared for was the amount of responses I receive, but more than that was the candid nature of these e-mails. People who wouldn't consult their own spouse about something personal were writing me to ask for advice. Amazing. Along with that surprise came the running theme of the column. It usually starts with a simple question, but always ends the same way, "...so Carmen, am I and is THIS normal?" There is the bottom line concern with the majority of my subscribers. They don't feel vexed over any thing out of the ordinary--they just want to know that they're not alone. If nothing else, this forum offers peace of mind and the opportunity to help others in the same situation. My subscribers never cease to amaze me with their capacity for assistance. No sooner does one reader write in with a question, than 100 are offering their advice, or as they say, "two cents."

While I love to help people and offer my advice with the best of intentions, I frequently caution my readers that I am not a licensed sex therapist or doctor. I am simply an enthusiast and very passionate about the subject. I strive to provide the most accurate information for my readers and thus never hesitate to research the various subjects. While I try to be as thorough as possible in my essays and replies, "Great Sexpectations" should not be taken in lieu of a professional's advice.

Do I plan to continue? Of course. Will I ever compete with the likes of the Peeps page? Maybe not, but I will always have a platform with your name on it when the time comes for you, too, to offer your own personal spin on matters of the heart. As always, I remain...

Devotedly yours,

Carmen

♀ Chapter One ♂
He Said, She Said

"Houston, we've got a problem…" Perhaps this declaration stands as one of the greatest understatements ever uttered, until you started dating. Apollo 13 was child's play next to some of your more famous omissions. If you can recall using such time-honored phrases such as, "Well if you don't know, I'm not going to say" or "NOTHING is bothering me!" then this is the chapter for you. Chapter one focuses on the most fundamental yet crucial aspects of any successful relationship--communication. I don't mean the standard head-nodding or grunts of acknowledgement you exchange in the hallway, either. I'm talking about really listening and engaging in meaningful dialogue. If I had a dime for every letter I received from a subscriber asking for help… yada, yada, yada! What constantly amazes me is how often we will ask someone outside of the relationship for advice rather than addressing the person it concerns.

Apparently it lies deep in the mind somewhere that your loved one must surely feel everything you feel, right? By the time we finally wake up and realize that there is no mind reading, we have to rethink our strategy. Communication should begin at the beginning, which is where most of the mistakes are made. In the beginning, everyone practices their best manners. Nobody wants to look too assertive or unpleasant, so you bite your lip for the sake of the team. Unfortunately the non-confrontational behavior comes back to haunt you because you've set a precedent. In order to look more agreeable, you've left your real opinions and feelings out of the equation. When you finally try to convey your feelings, your partner looks at you in abject amazement like "…and WHO are you?" Whoops! All this time you've been painting yourself in a rosy glow and avoiding the tougher subjects so when it finally happens, you look like you've got a serious case of the "Jekyll and Hyde Syndrome." Of course you can read body language and notice certain gestures (eye contact versus no eye contact), but this hardly scratches the surface. I find that clear communication is especially true when we have to discuss our sexual endeavors. For the sake of not hurting your partner's feelings, you avoid letting him or her know what really floats your boat and just accept what's offered, which leads to some serious trouble down the road. Imagine the horror when you find out that he/she detests the missionary position or the tongue-in-the-ear kiss.

Like the saying goes, you can't lock the barn door after the horse gets away because when he gets back, he'll be hostile, cold, and very hard to ride again. Okay that's not the expression, but it's my spin on an old classic. This chapter covers some of the basic strategies of effective communication, and not all of them entail verbal skills. For the sake of clarity, allow me to rephrase in a style that would make Frankenstein jealous: read chapter--words good!

Today's Topic: Getting to Know GS Readers

Sometimes I forget that the only reader comments you get to read are the ones that I furnish on Friday. In the meantime, I've had a chance to read them all, so today I wanted to take a moment to describe the typical subscriber topics and comments so we can all pause on the same page. It might surprise you to see how similar the concerns and personalities are for this column.

When I first decided to write this column, it was with both unbridled enthusiasm and a slight hesitation. It was my intention to bring some of the sensitive issues out of the closet and give them a forum where they could be discussed openly and without reservation. In terms of sexual content, there are millions of porn sites just waiting to be downloaded, so I wanted to target a more educated audience who was looking to ask questions or pose ideas that would be beneficial to everyone.

To my surprise, most of my readers are educated people with an open mind about human sexuality. This is not the column for perversion, so I guess I've weeded out the occasional extremist. What I find most surprising and refreshing is how honest my readers are. As some of you know, I sometimes will write to you directly for a quick clarification or reference, and I'm always amazed at how open you are about what you do, where you live, and what concerns you have about your sexuality and relationships. During the run of "Great Sexpectations," this is what I know about most of my readers:

1. Almost all of you write with specific concerns about your relationships. You either want to break up with your "first," be with your "first," or learn how to make things better with your current love. When I say better, it means that there's another division. That is those of you that want to know how to improve on an already great thing, and some of you have certain goals in mind.

For instance, I get thousands of letters from men and women wanting to know how or why they can achieve a vaginal orgasm. As I've said in the past, many of you equate vaginal orgasm as the ONLY one or the most important type to have. This couldn't be further from the truth.

Many women carry the majority of nerve endings in the clitoral area and therefore are more prone to this type of release. There is nothing wrong or abnormal about this, so don't worry. Just relax and enjoy the way your body works.

2. By far the next most popular request comes in equal amounts from both sexes concerning oral sex. I've lost count of how many of you feel intimidated or inept when it comes to oral stimulation, so I find myself going through back issues to see how often I can re-acquaint you with some of the more stimulating techniques. Often times this topic is treated with a certain amount of taboo, so many of these letters can be divided into what I call the "how can I get my partner to try oral sex on me" category. I'm still surprised at the amount of couples out there who have fallen into the giving/receiving pile only. Some of you give it; some of you get it, but many of you don't take turns. This would never fly with me, but if you're happy with this arrangement, who am I to argue? Okay, I won't argue, but I will push my vote for the 50/50 effort!

In this same category, I'd like to commend the thousands of you who write to me about improving or expanding your oral sex technique for the most admirable reason: to please your partner. Ladies, I know you'll be surprised by this, but the number of letters I get from male readers in this genre far outweigh the amount I get from you. This is based purely on my subscribers and nothing scientific. Please don't ask me to re-read all of the letters from Florida residents, either.

These letters almost always explain something very basic and simple. My male readers could care less about their own satisfaction if their partners aren't happy. Most of these men place the highest value and satisfaction on driving their lovers insane with pleasure and desire. Most of these men actually get off more on hearing this than having their own orgasms. Bravo!

3. This last type of letter usually addresses a perceived "problem," which usually is no problem at all. These letters address penis size, duration, shape, vaginal discomfort or painful intercourse, lack of

orgasm, discharge, nocturnal emissions, lack of sexual effort and so on. These are all legitimate concerns, and you should all know that NONE of you are alone. If there's a question or an insecurity out there, you've written it. I can sometimes be tongue-in-cheek, but I never dismiss these worries as small or insignificant. We are the most vulnerable and sensitive creatures on the planet when it comes to sex, and our confidence is easily shaken.

Have you ever seen an animal in the zoo cover his genitals in abject humiliation? No, sir! They carry on like Pamela and Tommy no matter how many people are watching because they don't have to care! I'm not suggesting public displays of nookie, just a healthy appreciation for what makes you unique. Now before I forget, the females who write to me about painful intercourse should be asking their doctors, not me. I know it exists, but I would never profess to know the physical reason behind your troubles.

There are, of course, other letters that I cherish which are the success stories. Some of you try something you read here and tell me how incredibly successful it was. Sometimes it takes a while, but thank you for trying again and especially for letting me in on it. As you can see, most of my readers are intelligent, solvent individuals with worthy contributions. Some of you chide and reject what I write which is perfectly acceptable, but do try it before you dismiss it. Above all, do not pass judgment on something just because it never happened to you or you never experienced it!

For the record, there IS such thing as female ejaculation, and NO it's not semen; it's lubricant in concentrated amounts. Speaking of F.E., I think I'll rerun that issue on page 103 for the know-it-alls who scoff. If you're a man who doubts, I understand, but if you've never had a vagina, you'll just have to trust me! Keep writing. Without your input this column would be nothing.

♡ ♡ ♡ ♡ ♡ Reader Comments ♡ ♡ ♡ ♡ ♡

Hiya, Carmen,

I am so glad that someone is trying to inform people about the way sex can be. After all the damage I'm sure TZ has done, we need more people like you. :-)

[TZ, our adult jokes editor, can be subdued, but it involves throwing raw meat at him first...it's not pretty.]

Dear Carmen,

Thank you for you. As far as God is concerned, I think you are filling a very important need for folks out here. I have always been told, "judge not." Thanks again.

I know you are very busy so, God bless you and have a nice day.

Dear Carmen,

I want to thank you for reminding us that sex is not just about getting together and "doing it."

Thanks!

Dear Carmen,

I absolutely love your articles! I have been looking everywhere to find something so open and honest! Keep up the great articles.

Carmen,

You're hot sweaty jungle monkey sex on a cold and rainy day. Your article is the warm tingly feeling in the midst of a down-pour of boring daily memos and news articles. Trudge forth, my little sexual soldier.

[Oh my...]

Today's Topic: What Women Like

As promised, I've decided to slow things down a bit and tackle some of the basics. While we're already familiar with the fact that men are from Mars and women are out shopping, it's crucial that we discuss some very important fundamental differences between the sexes. No, I'm not alluding to the fact that all men were born knowing how to make car sounds, or women inherently know how to "awwwwww" at baby showers. Don't dismiss this as beginner's material because without the bottom of the pyramid...

I'm sure this has been brushed over several times, but I was surprised at how many of my male friends were never instructed by a sister or close friend about the ground rules for intimacy. This is just a sketch, and I will be asking my readers to add to the list. Men and women have different preferences for sex and foreplay, but for my male audience I'll be repeating the phrase "slow, slow, and slow" until you're repeating this mantra in your sleep!

As a general rule, women fall in love with their minds while men fall with their eyes. It's no secret that men are more visually stimulated than women which means that men should work towards a cerebral surrender. If you doubt this, check out the stories about people falling in love online in my buddy's column, "Mook's Personals." In most cases both the men and women report how they fell head-over-heels based on what was heard and not seen.

Men prefer a fast rush to sex while women thrive on a slow and gradual approach. Most of this has to do with the female need to be RELAXED. If a woman is not relaxed, she would sooner clean the litter box before having sex. Women also thrive on the amount of attention they receive from their partners. One of the biggest complaints I've heard from almost every woman I know is that their men only touch them when they want sex. BIG TURNOFF! This approach makes a woman feel mechanical and automated. "It's like he wants to flip a switch without any thought and expects me to just swoon over his three seconds of attention." That approach should only be used with a bowling ball and not a woman.

Have I mentioned "slow, slow, slow" recently?

Most men love wet-tongue kisses in the ear; however, SOME women hate it. Please check with her first.

Women respond to gentle light touching, but men prefer deeper pressure. Most of this has to do with basic physiological differences, and of course there are exceptions to every rule. Men tend to be goal-oriented and charge to the orgasm. Women are far more intrigued with the journey, not the destination. Women like to know that they're worth the time and effort.

These are just a few of the differences, but if you can keep this in mind it will certainly help your efforts. As always, the most successful encounters take place between partners who express themselves clearly. Communication is still the best aphrodisiac. Drop me a line and tell me what you would add to this list.

♡ ♡ ♡ ♡ ♡ Reader Comments ♡ ♡ ♡ ♡ ♡

Dear Carmen,

Personally, one of the things that I want most from a sexual experience is to know that I am making HER happy. There is nothing worse than sexual guesswork. I need her to tell me what she likes and doesn't like so that I can know I'm doing something right. It's a male ego thing, I know, but I need that feeling that I'm doing it right, some affirmation, if you will. Sadly, yes, many men touch their women with only sex in mind.

Dear Carmen,

I laugh every time I hear, "He only touches me when he wants sex." I laugh because EVERY guy is guilty of this. We only touch our women when we want sex, because we ALWAYS want sex. Duh. "Verbosity leads to unclear, inarticulate things." - Vice President Al Gore, 11/30/96

[Affirmation well noted, my friend.]

Dear Carmen,

I am a female of 33 years, and I like things just a little rougher than most, not outright kinky or anything, but nibble, don't kiss, pull my hair, don't caress my head, that kind of thing, Men need to understand that this behavior is wanted in bed *after* the gentle foreplay is over with, NOT in the beginning. A person cannot just walk up and pull my hair and expect to turn me on, even though I love it rough. To satisfy, you still have to caress with the velvet glove to first peak my interest. Please pass this on to the male readers!

[Now here's a woman with a plan.]

Carmen:

Are you really a male?

[Uh, no. I wonder why this was asked! Any guesses out there?]

Dear Carmen,

In response to the reader who asked if you were a man. Here is my guess, being a man myself. There are two factors: the first is that we as men are STILL (I swear!) taught that "nice girls don't do THAT except to have babies or to get something." This is not directly taught, but it is strongly implied throughout our lives, so we have a very difficult time thinking of women as sexually hungry creatures. Yes, we lay them, but if she enjoys it, we men often come away with a feeling that we have either found the needle in the haystack, or that she is after something like a wedding ring, money, a place to live, or someone to take care of her. This contributes heavily to the distrust and resentment men often have of women.

The other factor is many of us learn about sex to an extent through letters published in "men's" magazines. Many of these soi-disant readers' letters are purported to be written by women, but we aren't fooled. We know that they were written by men. These two things combined often lead men to think that any time they run into a purportedly female sex columnist, it is actually a guy. (The mental image that comes to mind is of a balding, grossly obese guy whose wardrobe primarily consists of strappy t-shirts and green workpants, who doesn't shower or brush nearly often enough, smokes cheap, rank cigars, and couldn't get laid at a Nymphomaniac Empowerment Convention.)

While I am on the subject, something I have long wondered is why male erotica writers make a big deal out of bra cup size and other measurements, then try to convince the readers that they are female? Anyway, for the record, I am certain that you are female (and thank God!). Thanks for all the great info!

[Thanks for the vote of female confidence...and the wit! A Nymphomaniac Empowerment Convention? This one fractured me!]

Hello, Carmen,

To the guy who was taught that if a woman loves sex, she's after something--you're darn right, she's after something! She's after a man who can give her a passionate, erotic, wonderfully sensual experience. What else could she possibly want?

♡ ♡ ♡ ♡ ♡ ♡ ♡ ♡ ♡ ♡ ♡ ♡ ♡ ♡ ♡ ♡ ♡ ♡ ♡ ♡

Today's Topic: Don't Go Changin'

As usual, I draw my inspiration from a source greater than mere mortal wisdom. That's right, I'm referring to that all-powerful force called timing. It's a combination of that and the letters I receive asking some very poignant questions about typical concerns with no easy answers. I don't claim to have any answers, but I can always offer an interested opinion. Today's topic concerns the familiar phrase "Say what you mean and mean what you say." Easy enough? I think not...

Oh, all right! I apologize for the "Muzak" pun, but it fits the complaint of the week. This is dedicated to all of those who claim to know what they're looking for in a relationship, but change their story after a spell, when it's convenient.

Example A: She has a detailed outline of everything she deems important in a partner. He must have a sense of humor, practice good oral hygiene, and simply adore her mother. You know who she is; she's the one that provided a bio that closely describes your basic character profile, but after the first few dates you find yourself totally confused. While she's claiming one set of values, her behavior mirrors a different one. What you find out is that she really wants a man who is humorless, has bad breath, and would go out of his way to sell her mother to the nearest terrorist. You're left with more than a few questions and a bad hangover. I'm here to ease your troubled mind. Ready? IT WASN'T YOU!

You've fallen into the Bermuda Triangle of relationships, and Captain Steubing isn't there to guide your happy ass off the Loveboat (but Carmen is). This is actually more common than you think. Many well-rounded individuals get caught up in this syndrome where they're afraid of rejection or worried that they'll never find the enigma they truly desire so they pad the zone by claiming to want some body that has all of the "popular" traits. These alleged traits are chosen to reflect a glowing light on their demeanor, but it usually backfires. Imagine how refreshing it would be to meet someone who offers an honest request.

Yes, we all know someone that makes us feel like the fluffy glowing epicenter of the universe blah, blah, and blah. Let's look beyond the giddy stage into the grit that makes up everyday life. When you're all alone, what do you REALLY want? Here's an example of desire that goes beyond good dental work:

Example B: I (insert your name here) truly desire somebody who is politically incorrect, laughs out of context, makes incredible coleslaw, has a few scars to prove he/she's experienced adversity, isn't looking for perfection, would never leave wet towels on the new comforter, enjoys the simple things, lets me watch black and white "B" movies starring Basil Rathbone, admits that roller coasters make them feel horny, picks up the doggie doo-doo, isn't afraid to take chances, secretly listens to disco, sticks to their exercise routine unless they only want a carton of Ben & Jerry's, admits total ignorance about the wine, but still smells the cork to be a sport, and above all, doesn't require constant stimulation by vegging out at all of the appropriate and inappropriate times. Gasp, pant, wheeze!

Take a breath. That's not the profile you hear, is it? You're so used to hearing the Oprah Book Club response that you lost touch with a few tenets of the human condition, primarily that you are human and come with a few conditions.

My rant is aimed at only one goal. Say what you mean and save the rest of us a ton of trouble. If your ideal mate resembles Alan Greenspan or Wilma Flintstone, embrace your true desires...unless you really desire a cartoon, in which case we'll have a whole new topic to discuss!

♡ ♡ ♡ ♡ ♡ Reader Comments ♡ ♡ ♡ ♡ ♡

Dear Carmen,

I loved the column. Betty is really more my type, but I guess Wilma would do. Hugs and kisses

[I think she'd go for it, too!]

Dear Carmen,

I'm not sure if you answer general dating questions, but I have one that has perplexed my girlfriends and me for years! Why do guys change once they start dating you? It's like they almost feel that they don't have to try once they have you as their girlfriend.

Before, they're tripping over themselves to get you to go on dates and try to impress you. What, if anything, can we do to get our guys back to this predating way of acting? Or is it a lost cause for us to dream?

[Absolutely not. You don't stop eating just because you know how, do you? Keep feeding your relationship or it will stagnate.]

Dear Carmen,

I love my man. He is the sweetest and most passionate man I know when we are alone, but in front of people, not just friends but even strangers, he can be a total ass with no manners.

Growing up with two sisters you would think that he would have a clue as to how to treat a lady, as in introducing you to an acquaintance, waiting until you get up before bolting out of the restaurant, holding a door, etc. Is there an obedience school for men?

[If there were, I'd run it and retire early.]

Today's Topic: Playing Fair

The nature of writing this column can sometimes lend itself to the "he said, she said" syndrome, but recently somebody wrote in about making new efforts in the bedroom. This more than merits attention because how do we approach our loving partners when we want to keep things fresh?

Lately I've concentrated solely on techniques for PC muscle control which is important, but it's strictly for mechanical/physical improvement. When it comes to relationships, there is (should be) a delicate balance between both physical and emotional needs. When you were first dating, you spent a great deal of time grooming your intellectual, romantic, and sexual desires. Each attribute requires respect and attention, but sometimes things change. What happens when you both notice the cooling period in the bedroom?

Most of the emails I read detail the problems that start when one partner is reluctant to talk about changes in the bedroom. Anyone who has ever been intimate knows that keeping things passionate is critical. Once (if) you stop making those extra efforts, stop experimenting or slack off in the foreplay department, you've got a problem. Making love can start to feel less satisfying or worse: ordinary. I've lost count of how many emails my readers have sent expressing the utter defeat and frustration they feel when things get stale, but the real issue is "what should I do, how can I change this?"

It's pretty obvious when sex needs to be fine-tuned, so finding the right approach for your relationship depends on how strong the foundation is with your mate. To be frank, both partners are painfully aware when things are cooling down without saying a word (the beauty of nonverbal communication). It's the look in your eyes, the intensity of your touching, the lack of caressing, or the infrequency of your relations. For most, the toughest part is finding a way to approach the subject. If conversation is not your strongest suit, try a subtle yet noticeable change the next time you make love. I'm not suggesting anything obtuse or ridiculous (put the goat DOWN!). Try a new position, location, body oil, or approach. Trust me, it will be noticed.

After you're finished, it should be a natural progression towards opening a dialogue. "So...what was THAT all about?" might be one way to start negotiations. Progress towards discussing what you liked, what you look forward to, and what you'd like to try. You're not hurting anyone's feelings, you're just sharing your honest feelings about what would spice things up in the bedroom. Please understand that it's not only to the benefit of one...it's always for both. Who said, "There's no such thing as a great lover, just great partners?" True. Nobody should fear taking their relationship to a higher level.

If this conversation is met with some hesitation or reluctance, don't get irritated. Before you assume that your partner is being stubborn, lazy, or power hungry, stop and ask what he/she is so afraid of. Chances are someone read into the conversation and thought their prowess was being attacked, or they were being blamed for the lack of excitement.

This is where most negotiations come screeching to a halt. As soon as one of you feels like you're being blamed, hurt feelings take over and you'll adopt an overly defensive posture. This is where the "if you're so bored, why don't you find somebody else" comments start to surface. This is also the point where communication breaks down, and nothing constructive happens.

The other possibility is that you both agree that something should change, but one partner wants the other to do all of the work. This sometimes sounds like, "I'm already trying everything I know; you're going to have to try something new." Wrong again. Pointing the accusatory finger or using your best passive-aggressive tactic is also destructive. You'll only enrage or frustrate your partner. This is also known as a "self-fulfilling prophecy." As soon as you dare someone to fail, see how fast they oblige you. If you thought that reverse psychology was the key, you'll probably wind up disappointed again.

You have to decide if you're in it together or for your own satisfaction. Truthfully, most couples want to please each other above and beyond all other needs. Don't forget that sexual intimacy is the most vulnerable you'll ever be. If you remember to approach changes with tenderness and respect, you'll succeed beyond your expectations. Good luck, and let me know if you've ever been in this situation.

♡ ♡ ♡ ♡ ♡ Reader Comments ♡ ♡ ♡ ♡ ♡

Hi, Carmen,

I have been reading your newsletter every day and think it's great. I have a small question, though. I am 19 and have always had trouble communicating with my partner about any sort of serious subject. But my new girlfriend is wonderful, and we communicate well. We've been together for a while, and I want to bring up the issue of different positions, etc. to keep our sex life interesting and fresh.

I don't know how to bring it up or what to talk about. Should I bring it up and be awkward and just take the initiative and do it? It's not like we are stale or anything, but I just want to make sure that it never happens. Thanks again and keep up the great work!

[Honesty is a simple, gentle solution. Tell her what you told me and don't be afraid.]

Dear Carmen,

My wife of four years isn't very adventurous. She hates foreplay (giving and receiving) and only likes sex missionary or doggie style. I have been frustrated for quite some time, and she knows how I feel about these issues, but she won't hear of it. She's stuck in her ways. Her ways make it hard for me to bring her to the next pleasure level and very hard for her reach the first orgasm. I've told her, shown her, etc. how I can make things for her, but she refuses any teachings from me. What can I do in these circumstances? Desperately seeking help.

[If she's resisting change, ask her what her real fears are, then decide on a mutual plan of action. Support her, don't threaten her.]

Dear Carmen,

I just want to start off by saying I LOVE YOUR COLUMN! I have been married for almost four years. I love my hubby with all my heart. I have tried talking him into to trying new things with me sexually. He doesn't seem very interested in this. All he wants is missionary or me on top. Do you have any suggestions on how I can talk to him about this? I am willing to try any suggestions. I have a very high sex drive, and honestly sex is getting kind of dull. Could you please help me? -- Desperate in California

[Clear communication is crucial; you MUST develop this first.]

Carmen,

I have only been a subscriber for long enough to read two or three columns so far, and what I have read I must say is great. I only have one question for you, and it will pertain of course to just how adventurous you are, Carmen. Will you marry me?

[Ahhhhh! My first proposal. How wonderful!]

Today's Topic: The Madonna Syndrome and Systems of Power

Perhaps this sounds familiar. Your relationship used to be a firestorm of passionate encounters complete with spontaneous playtime, romantic dinners, and entire weekends spent in bed. As you continued down the usual path toward matrimony and children, something changed. I don't just mean your responsibilities, but the dynamic between you and your partner turned a corner after you had children. It's called the Madonna Syndrome, and it has the potential to destroy a once-healthy relationship.

While I don't lend too much credence to Freud's psychology, he managed to pinpoint certain phenomenon to the individual's concept of sexuality. One of the most perplexing aspects of the human condition surrounds the many roles we have to sustain. If you look at the average female, she could hold as many as six roles at once. She could be a sister, a daughter, a cousin, a niece, a lover, and a mother all at the same time. Most of these positions exist without being in direct conflict, right? I have no trouble being a daughter and a sister at the same time, but the dynamic changes when you have to be the mother and the lover simultaneously. The same applies to a man when he becomes both the father and the lover.

For some couples the introduction of a child can be a very positive, well-rounded compliment to an already fulfilling relationship. For others, a child entails redefining one's identity as well as the power structure that was previously in place. Some of your letters outline two of the most common problems that accompany parenthood.

The first example of the Madonna Syndrome affects the woman. In the beginning she was your muse, partner, and sexual dynamo. After the child is born, she instinctively learns the maternal skills, but along with that, she surrenders her sexual self. Why? Because she has immersed herself in the role of mother/nurturer at the expense of her sexual identity. For some women, the focus of motherhood becomes so intense that it creates an identity conflict. The mother identity becomes the primary role, and she now sees herself in a different light.

Perhaps you'll notice her wardrobe choices are now leaning toward unstructured, soft textured fabrics. Her choice of cosmetics changes, or she has stopped wearing them. I'm not referring to the stage after childbirth where she's still too big to wear her old clothes, either. The bottom line is that she now LOOKS like a mother and not your lover. This is how she views herself, and she has trouble integrating her sexual self with her maternal self. This can be traumatic for the husband because he has to deal with sexual rejection for the first time in the relationship.

The second example of the Madonna Syndrome is similar to the first, only it's the man who has trouble adjusting to the situation. He used to have a primal sexual attraction to his mate until the child is born. He now may feel that lust is inappropriate, so he may begin to distance himself sexually. He may compensate by consuming himself in the daddy and provider roles, but his feelings about his lover have changed drastically. Physical displays of affection in front of the child are discouraged, as well as in the bedroom. His major conflict stems from his inability to see his partner as a lover now that she is a mother. Some men equate all mothers with their own, so intimacy may now feel awkward.

All couples tackle a new identity with children, but for some the transition is rough. Many of you have written to me expressing anxiety over these sexual changes, but unfortunately there is no easy answer. For some, professional counseling is the best answer if you feel there is a need for intervention. For others, it simply entails a waiting period while you both adjust to your new roles.

The foundation for any successful relationship depends on communication, but it's important to know that you aren't alone. I encourage you to write about your experience with the Madonna Syndrome because everyone deals with it in different degrees. I am not married nor do I have children, so I think it would be more productive for me to publish your letters about this so we can cover it together. As always, I thank you for your interest and ideas!

♡ ♡ ♡ ♡ ♡ Reader Comments ♡ ♡ ♡ ♡ ♡

Dearest Carmen,

I've been married for two years and have one child. After I had our daughter, I completely have lost interest in sex. I feel like he doesn't appreciate me for being the mother of his first born. I feel like he just doesn't find me sexy anymore (even though he tells me all the time how beautiful I am).

I find it hard to even get aroused, even though he's still as gorgeous as the day he first stopped to help me change my car tire. I want romance, and I want intimacy. When I explain that to him, he ignores me. It's just a Catch-22 situation. To try and solve our problems, he's gone away for a few days. This is the first time we've been away from each other since we got married. We'll see how it turns out!

Dear Carmen,

Your article yesterday really tweaked me. I have been married for just under six years. My wife and I have two children (a three-and-a-half year old and a ten month old). After our first child, our sex life did take a small downturn. Since the birth of our second child, sex is almost as rare as a quiet house (children playing, crying, making noise, not adults yelling at each other). We still have a strong and loving relationship with each other, but lately something is missing.

I have always been the "experimental type," and I try to bring in new things and ideas to our lovemaking. I never bring in something that I know will shock my wife or suggest anything that I know she will not do. I have told her on several occasions what I would like to do and what I would like for her to do, but it is of no use anymore.

For example, last night I was performing oral sex on my wife. I was playing around a bit by bringing her to the edge of an orgasm then slowing down or changing my area of focus. I did this a few times, then she basically stopped me, rolled over and said to either finish it or get away. To be honest, I was crushed. That was the last straw. I got up from what I was doing and went back to my side of the bed to go to sleep. I consider myself a giver. I want to satisfy my wife in all ways sexually. I am more pleased when I know I have brought my wife to orgasm. I know that sometimes she doesn't orgasm, and that is okay (as long as it is not too often).

I have asked her what she wants me to do, and she just says that she doesn't know. I don't know what to do. Last night ended in her crying and me not happy. We tried to discuss what was going on in our sexual relationship but got nowhere. I told her that I want to make her happy, but I need a clue to what it is that she wants. Again, we were not mad or yelling at each other, we were both disappointed. Carmen, HELP! What am I to do? Where do I go from here? Thanks!

Dear Carmen,

My husband and I experienced this to some degree after the birth of both of my children. However, it was only during the nursing stage. My husband and I both felt my breasts were "off limits" sexually as long as I was nursing. We felt the breasts belonged solely to the children as long as they nursed.

Today's Topic: The Art of Staying in Love

I read that the average person suffers through at least five failed relationships before marriage, and those who make it down the aisle find themselves divorcing 50% of the time. Pretty grim, huh? Most people are capable of falling in love, but how many stay in love?

Many have written to me about watching your relationship go from the "pants on fire" stage to the "PBS documentary" phase. The truth is that it takes patience, understanding, and a really solid foundation to make a relationship survive the long haul. Perhaps I'm reaching for the obvious, but I can't stress enough how important a solid friendship is when it comes to making a long-term relationship succeed. Try to remember what your first few months together were like. If you are like most couples, you gave your partner undivided attention. You probably both really listened to each other in an effort to find out what they were all about. This practice should continue long after the courtship.

Toni Morrison made the comment that a child looks to see if your face lights up when they enter the room because these physical signals validate the child. Why should it be any different with your lover? It shouldn't. When you stop doing everything you're involved with to let your partner know that they are the BEST part of your day, it can change the entire mood of an evening together.

Many of you have written about how he/she just stopped trying after the initial pursuit. Shame on anyone who takes their partner for granted! If you find yourself in this situation, you have to change the behavior by letting them know that indifference is not acceptable. Real friends continue to work at their relationships which means sharing your heart, exercising patience, and allowing themselves to just feel. Part of what keeps couples in love is the trust they develop knowing that their partner will be there unconditionally. Big word, unconditional, but it's crucial for any real relationship to last.

If you're in that mode of moving through your relationship on automatic pilot, STOP immediately and make those changes. Start by turning off the TV! Television has sucked the life blood out of many an evening. Instead, go for a walk and just enjoy your time together. Play cards, go for a drive, play Twister; I don't care what you do as long as it involves one-on-one attention. There's no excuse for ever living passively. Yes, I know the kids have to eat and homework needs to be completed, but anything important is worth making time for, capiche? It's usually the simple things that matter most in the end. Personally, I'm a huge fan of blackouts. What can you do without electricity? Pretend you're Amish and go to town!

♡ ♡ ♡ ♡ ♡ Reader Comments ♡ ♡ ♡ ♡ ♡

Dear Carmen,

I am a 74-year-old woman and have been sexually rejuvenated. When I playfully let my husband know, we immediately tried again. After years of not practicing, there was no success for either of us reaching climax. Surprise, surprise. Our physician suggested Viagra. The pill was successful in that he now does have the erection, but is unable to climax. I did, but only once. He tells me it does not really matter to him. It is really wonderful to just cuddle and feel close to each other again. This is true; still, it would be more than nice if we could both go over the top together again. I tried the various suggestions in your more recent messages, but I want to do more, for both of us. Anything else to try? I enjoy your column immensely. Do you realize how huge your readership is? Here I am, a 74-year-old, married 54 years, still learning new things from you. I really do appreciate and thank you.

[I think if you are still willing to take your time and express yourselves sexually, you're an inspiration to the real spirit of love. Bless you both!]

♀ Chapter Two ♂

Recipes for Love

This just in: everyone eats! Not only do we all eat, some of us actually enjoy it. When dealing with the three basic urges hunger, thirst, and sex, can you think of anything more sensible than combining all at once? Certain foods contain elements that enhance or stimulate our amorous nature, but the beauty of using aphrodisiac foods lies in the simplicity of nature. Food is associated with every event of our lives. Holidays, weddings, birthdays, anniversaries, and even death are surrounded by food. Why should romance be excluded? These recipes remind us that romance involves all of the senses, not just the obvious ones.

Many classic scenes of erotica have taken place around food. The movie *91/2 Weeks* features a feast where Kim Basinger finds herself blindfolded and fed by hand in front of the fridge on the floor by a very taunting Mickey Rourke. He dangles his offerings right out of her reach and at times covers her in cherry juice while licking it off of her body. Sounds pretty good, right? Speaking of cherries, if anyone remembers David Lynch's "Twin Peaks," it features a talented Sherilyn Fenn taking a whole cherry into her mouth, and after a tawdry smile, she spits out just the stem, tied in a knot. I can't tell you how many women I saw trying this out in public after that episode aired. They had the attention of every man within eye shot! The idea that food is both a need and oral gratification means that incorporating two very pleasurable events will always yield great results. It's also a gesture that entails feeding both the body and the soul. Choose from your favorites from chocolate to honey to pine nuts and try your own nine and a half ...minutes!

Today's Topic: Aphrodisiacs

Look out! I feel like cooking today, and my poor dinner guest has no idea that he's going to be at the mercy of my culinary Kung Fu. Yes, I'm talking about aphrodisiacs in every edible form. So hang on to your pots and pans...it's going to be bumpy ride. For the benefit of the beginners, it's an adjective meaning "arousing sexual desire." I realize that for some, this entails a six-pack and a porno magazine, but for my more refined readers, allow me to familiarize you with some of my favorite food groups. Most of these taunting edibles have been utilized throughout history and have a very successful track record. Cheese Whiz and SPAM are not on the list. I'm talking about real, unprocessed foods.

The most successful love potions include the following foods: artichokes, asparagus, avocado, basil, black beans, chilies, chocolate, coffee, figs, grapes, honey, libations (cocktails), olives, oysters, pine nuts, rosemary, strawberries, and some edible flowers. There are many more if you include some of our more popular spices, but I'm going to start with one of my favorite recipes.

Arabian Couscous with Pine Nuts and Raisins
[Best served while scantily clad on a sultry night.]

1 tablespoon unsalted butter
1/2 small onion, minced
1/2 medium carrot, diced
1/2 cup couscous
1 cup chicken stock
1/4 cup dark raisins (soaked in white wine)
2 tablespoons pine nuts toasted
1/2 juiced lemon
salt and pepper to taste

Heat butter in a saucepan. Add the onion and carrot; sauté until translucent, about five minutes. Add stock and raisins; raise heat to high and bring to a boil. Add couscous, stir briefly, cover, and remove from heat. Let stand five mintes. Stir in pine nuts and lemon juice. Season with salt and pepper.

I'll contribute more delicacies in the future, but I'm very interested in what works for my readers. Do any of you have recipes that get results? Please email, and I'll gladly publish your ideas in a future issue. Until then, keep your burners hot!

♡ ♡ ♡ ♡ ♡ Reader Comments ♡ ♡ ♡ ♡ ♡

Hey, Carmen,

I love your newsletter. Great piece on aphrodisiacs, but I have only one small problem. The Arabian Couscous looks like a great recipe, but my girlfriend is a vegetarian. Any way around the chicken stock? Thanks and keep up the good work.

[I, too, am a vegetarian; just use vegetable broth. It's really great!]

Carmen,

I love your column, but I do have one comment about the man who said the way to a mans heart is through his stomach. A rather boisterous female friend of mine said the best way to a man's heart is through his rib cage. LOL I think she would never really get that close to a man, nor one to her! Just a thought!

Oh, I am a great cook, and I also love a great cook in the kitchen with me. It carries to the bedroom in a lot more ways than most imagine!

♡ ♡ ♡ ♡ ♡ ♡ ♡ ♡ ♡ ♡ ♡ ♡ ♡ ♡ ♡ ♡ ♡ ♡ ♡

Today's Topic: Asparagus Frittata

As part of my continued devotion toward great sex and good living, it's time once again for another visit to Carmen's kitchen. Today's aphrodisiac of choice is asparagus. While summer quickly dwindles away, I am reminded of how fleeting seasonal vegetables are, so we better use them while they're still available.

One of you wrote me asking how to prepare the couscous recipe without chicken stock, and my answer was to replace it with vegetable broth instead. I am also a vegetarian, but I still prepare meat dishes for my friends. This may be eaten alone or prepared with a meat if you so choose. The beauty of this recipe is that it's light enough to be served on a hot summer night with a light white wine, and it won't leave you feeling bloated and sluggish (a certain death for romance and passion).

3 eggs beaten
2 tablespoons chopped basil
1 clove garlic, finely chopped
2 tablespoons grated parmesan cheese
1/4 pound thin asparagus
2 tablespoons olive oil
basil leaves for garnish

Combine the eggs, basil, garlic, and parmesan in a bowl. Season with salt and pepper. Let stand for 30 minutes. Trim the ends of the asparagus, and steam in a basket until tender but still bright green. Combine with a few drops of olive oil, and keep warm. Heat the remaining olive oil in a large skillet over medium-high heat. Pour a ladle full of egg mixture into the pan. Swirl around in the pan and lower the heat to medium. When the frittata turns opaque, flip it over and cook the other side until lightly browned. Repeat with the other frittata. Divide the asparagus into two bunches. Roll each bunch in a frittata, and garnish with basil leaves and cheese.

Of course you know how to serve this, right? Candles, great music, and flowers on the table make for a picture-perfect setting, but if you really want results try wearing a sheer apron...and a smile!

♡ ♡ ♡ ♡ ♡ Reader Comments ♡ ♡ ♡ ♡ ♡

Dear Carmen,

I agree with you about combining cooking, dining and romance. Sharing the tastes off each others' plates, feeding each other, conversation, eye contact, smiles, and don't forget the ever-sensual hands and mouth. It is a metaphor for sex and sets the stage for an incredible evening of intimacy and sharing. A couple that's uninhibited with trying new things and shares the taste of their meal with their partner exudes sexual compatibility and their desire to taste and please the other in a variety of ways. I learned this from a special relationship that I had. I wouldn't settle for someone without the same qualities of spontaneity and sensuality I experienced before. You're right--not everyone gets it. I enjoy your column and have shared it with special men in my life. Figure this out: one guy who was an especially picky eater was intimidated by your column and that I subscribed to it. He's history!

[Gees, threatened by a column? Too many issues there!]

Carmen,

No, a thousand nos to asparagus before any oral sex. There is a stink to the urine after eating asparagus and is still pungent the next morning, although to a lesser degree. It's more than just the urine; it's in the vaginal mucus, too.

♡ ♡ ♡ ♡ ♡ ♡ ♡ ♡ ♡ ♡ ♡ ♡ ♡ ♡ ♡ ♡ ♡ ♡ ♡

Today's Topic: Food for Football

As you know, I try to cover all aspects of sexuality including the culinary contributions. In response to the "gentleman" who voiced his disapproval over the aphrodisiac recipes, give them a try before you dismiss the idea. You never know what you will enjoy until you try it.

I can't think of anything more appealing than watching a man take the time to prepare a romantic meal (not to mention the sexy apron)! Today I have a different twist that I am sure you will enjoy.

The letters have already started:

> Dear Carmen,
>
> My husband and I both work, plus we have children which takes up most of our time. I'm trying to squeeze a little romantic time into the schedule, but my nemesis known as "Monday Night Football" has reared its ugly head again.
>
> I've tried distracting him from the game with some of the most outrageous outfits, but nothing seems to sway his focus. Do you have any suggestions?
>
> Signed, NFL (No Fun Lovin')

Sports run deep in the heart of many men, and if you're involved with a hard-core enthusiast, you probably know that it's futile to fight. If you know the seasons because of the sport on television, may I suggest making the game more of an event instead of a matrimonial grudge match? Football season does not have to signal the end of romantic affairs until January. Instead, try incorporating two of the most powerful aphrodisiacs (black beans and chilies) in one football-friendly dish. Good luck!

Black Bean Chili

1/2 pound ground chuck

1/2 pound chorizo sausage cut up

1 cup dried black beans, soaked overnight

3 cups water

1 rib of celery, chopped

1 small red bell pepper, chopped

2 tomatoes, peeled and chopped

1 medium carrot, chopped

1 medium onion, chopped

1 tablespoon minced garlic

2 tablespoons white wine vinegar

1/2 cup beer

1/2 teaspoon cayenne pepper

2 tablespoons ground chilies

sour cream for garnish

Brown the ground chuck and chorizo in a skillet; drain. Rinse and drain the soaked beans. Combine the beans and water in a large pot. Bring to a boil over medium heat. Add the red pepper, onion, celery, tomatoes, carrot, garlic, vinegar, beer, cayenne pepper, and chilies to the beans. Simmer, covered, for 1 1/2 hours or until beans are tender. Add the ground chuck and chorizo sausage. Simmer covered, for one hour more. Garnish with sour cream. Serve with rice or tortilla chips.

I think most men will choose the tortilla chips over the rice, don't you? I'm not suggesting that you get carried away and serve dinner in a cheerleader outfit. It's all about sharing. If you make the effort to make football season a joy rather than a tragedy, he is sure to respond favorably. If not, make it a girls' night out with the other football widows, and let him make his own dinner! Enjoy the chili!

♡ ♡ ♡ ♡ ♡ Reader Comments ♡ ♡ ♡ ♡ ♡

Dear Carmen,

Keep a man's stomach full and his prostate empty, and you will have a happy man.

[Pithy little phrase; thanks!]

Dear Carmen,

My grandmother has a plaque in her kitchen (has been there since I was a child) that states, "Kissin' don't last but cookin do!" I am a chef and can vouch for that! Thanks

Dear Carmen,

I don't know if you ever heard this one. My grandmother told me one time, "The best way to keep a man happy is if his stomach is full and his balls are empty." It seems that it is important to have his tummy full first, before the other "dessert" happens.

I look forward to your emails and learn about things all the time. I usually learn something new that I thought I had already experienced *and* mastered. However, it's always refreshing to know something new about ourselves and our bodies.

From one of your faithful readers

Dear Carmen,

I do not know about the rest of the male population of this planet, but the greatest sexual expieriences of my life have all begun with a fantastic meal. Thank you for the great newsletter!

Today's Topic: Great Cook or Temptress in the Bedroom?

I'll see if you can answer this bit of trivia. If given the choice between marrying a woman who is a really great cook or one who is fabulous in the bedroom, what percentage of men voted for the great cook? You may be surprised by the results, but please read on, and we will get through the guesses.

Well, the answer is 30%. If given the choice between a devil in the sheets or a great cook, 30% of the male respondents chose the great cook. I think there's more to this aphrodisiac stuff than meets the eye. I think it has something to do with feeling decadent, maintaining good health, and possibly the atmosphere. When all that is finally in place, you feel...amorous.

This just in: tomatoes are being touted as a great food for maintaining male health. It has been proven that tomatoes keep arteries clear, blood pressure in order, and actually work to prevent prostate cancer. For those of you who have been reading this since June, you know that the prostate and the PC muscle have a common mission: to keep the blood flowing to your penis as well as maintaining erections.

Knowing all of that, why wouldn't you want to eat well?

I've decided to combine one of my favorite aphrodisiacs (basil) with the highly effective tomato in order to satisfy the 30% who would like the great cook, along with the rest who would just like the amorous side-effect of the basil. I'm not sure who said it first (I'll check my email from my readers about this), but a very dear man just reminded me that the way to man's heart is through his stomach...among other things. So, surprise him with the following recipe for bruchetta and good luck!

Today's Favorite: Bruchetta

It comes in many forms, but don't bother without fresh ingredients.

10 plum tomatoes (seeds squeezed out and diced)
3/4 cup freshly washed basil leaves (minced)
2 cloves garlic minced
1/3 cup balsamic vinegar
1/4 cup extra virgin (no pun intended) olive oil
1/4 cup merlot
kosher salt to taste
dash of pepper
one loaf European baguette style bread

It is crucial to use fresh everything, but what really matters with this dish is the marinade time. After you combine all of the above, you have to let it sit out at room temperature for at least two hours. Before you serve, cut the bread into 1/2-inch rounds and cover a baking sheet with the rounds. Spray the bread with olive oil (infused is always good) and bake at 350 degrees until crispy (about 20 minutes). You can spray the bread with just olive oil, or you could sprinkle it with parmesan cheese as well. The idea is to make the bread rounds crispy so the tomatoes and the juice have a firm surface to rest on.

What makes this such a perfect recipe is its ability to travel well. All ingredients are served at room temperature so you can throw the bread rounds in a bag, throw the tomatoes in a plastic container and take it on a picnic. Because there's already red wine in the marinade, may I suggest serving this with a cabernet or a merlot? It's also one of those fun foods you can assemble individually and feed to your partner...very slowly. There's plenty of juice so you'll have plenty of fingers to lick.

I feel sad for those who have never incorporated dining with romance. They must exist because I'll get those narrow-minded emails that read something like "Enough with the food already, talk about oral sex!"

Poor misguided soul, he/she missed the whole point behind the art of seduction or the subtle joy of anticipating the moment. I know I've said this before, but its about more than the genitals! Make love with your mind, your food, and your very important silent moments. Silence you say? Yup. I think I'm about due right now.

♡ ♡ ♡ ♡ ♡ Reader Comments ♡ ♡ ♡ ♡ ♡

Dear Carmen:

I've been reading your articles for months and must agree on this: food and love definitely go together! Bruchetta and insalata caprese are two of my favorites and are an excellent appetizer to a lovemaking session. It is obvious that you should not eat heavily before attempting to make love; it not only makes you sleepy but could be dangerous. You can always eat lightly before and resume eating afterwards because making love generally makes you hungry. Thanks for your unique way of looking at sexuality and woman-man relationships. It is a refreshing oasis in a world of increasing materialism and bad taste.

Carmen, I thought you might like this: "Garden Tips" about tomatoes.

A beautiful woman loved growing tomatoes, but couldn't seem to get her tomatoes to turn red. One day while taking a stroll, she came upon a gentleman neighbor who had the most beautiful garden full of huge red tomatoes. The woman asked the gentleman, "What do you do to get your tomatoes so red?" The gentleman responded, "Twice a day I stand in front of my tomato garden and expose myself, and my tomatoes turn red from blushing so much." Well, the woman was so impressed, she decided to try doing the same thing to her tomato garden to see if it would work. Twice a day for two weeks she exposed herself to her garden. One day the gentleman was passing by and asked the woman, "By the way, how did you make out? Did your tomatoes turn red?" "No," she replied, "but my cucumbers are enormous."

♀ Chapter Three ♂
Stairway to Heaven

It can be as simple as a note in your lunch or a casual caress to a cheek with the back of your fingers, but one thing remains true; fabulous endings only happen with fabulous beginnings. I've tried very hard to explain foreplay as something more than the prescribed ritual of kiss-kiss-kiss-squeeze-squeeze-unzip...

Not this time! Foreplay is a true art form and very much deserves to be treated as such. If you want to treat this as a metaphor, think about foreplay as a job resume. You are detailing your skills and everything that you intend to bring to the job. Look at where I trained! I am great at multi-tasking and problem solving, too. I am a self-starter and rarely miss a deadline! I am proficient with my hands and my mind so there are few tasks I can't tackle with dazzling results. My strengths are creative strategies, patience, and I'm very flexible when it comes to spontaneous projects.

I don't know about you, but I would hire this person for some job (if there were no positions open, I would find one). The energy and importance you place on foreplay says a great deal about the kind of lover you are going to be.

In addition to this, the longer you engage in foreplay, the more relaxed and aroused you will both be, but especially the woman. Now, can you think of better reason to prolong the anticipation? I sure can't.

Today's Topic: Sent by Scent

Sometimes shopping can be a real eye opener. I'm not like other women when it comes to doing battle in the department stores. I'm more like General Patton; I know what I need, I plan my route, I go in and get out with a "take no prisoners" attitude. Usually, that is. While I was helping a friend in need complete some last-minute shopping, we ended up taking a trip through the store, nose first.

It doesn't happen too often, but I was completely caught off guard in the men's fragrance section. I wasn't even sampling the dangerous little bottles when the floor dropped out from under me. It was fragrance that stopped me cold. I had shivers, shakes, and a few spins for good measure. I couldn't place it in the first second, but the next second it was all over. It was a scent worn by an ex-boyfriend from years ago, and yet it was like I just smelled this yesterday. I know someone out there has had this experience, right?

Not only did I remember the smell, but I got all moonie and gushy right there in the store. I think I mumbled something incoherent to the salesman, but he was a credit to his career. He saw the stupefied look on my face (yes, I was listening to our homeboys, Disturbed) and offered the name of the fragrance immediately. He probably thought I was going to buy a case to bathe in, and he would have been right, but I am on a budget!

I was absolutely consumed with the scent for the rest of the evening, when all of a sudden, it dawned on me that the last few men I've dated do not wear cologne or aftershave. Suddenly, this is a problem. One small splash of cologne reduced me to a quivering mass of wanton hysteria. If I was so easily seduced, I wondered, then how many of my wonderful readers are doing without this perk?

I'm not saying it has to be anything heavy or musky. Sometimes a great shower gel is all you need, but what a difference! My current love uses Lever, but some of my previous lovers would splash a little cologne on before a dinner date (movie and a pizza on the couch) and WOW! I forgot how primal scent can be.

Here's your homework. Try using a few new scents without telling your partner to see how quickly it gets noticed. Remember to go lightly on the pulse points: behind the ears, the nape of the neck, the crook of your arm, behind your knees, between your breasts, or anywhere else you fancy. This goes a long way in the great sex nonverbal cue department, too. Even if you are cooking dinner or doing laundry, there's something about a subtle fragrance that says, "How about it?"

It's also important to remember that not all scents mix well with your body chemistry. Something might smell great in a bottle, but turn to vinegar on you. Similarly, a scent may smell great on a friend, but react differently on you. Try them while you are alone at first. If you don't like the smell, no amount of praise from your partner is going to change that. Choose something that feels right and smells how you want. If you're wearing something that you personally find sexually arousing, it's going to go far with potential or current partners.

Start with something really small like baby lotion and work your way up. It's too important to forget. Just as an aside, I got a call from an ex-boyfriend the other day that said he still thinks of me every time he smells a certain perfume I used to wear. What a kick! Someone still remembers me the way I remembered Mr. Nudge-wink. Now that I've reminded you about this, let the fragrances flow, but not too heavy. Write and tell me your favorite scent! Does just the scent of a boyfriend's cologne send chills downs your spine? Tell me aout it. More importantly, what do they make you do?

♡ ♡ ♡ ♡ ♡ Reader Comments ♡ ♡ ♡ ♡ ♡

Dear Carmen,

Oh, this one really hit the nail on the head! Fragrance is something that really turns me on, and when I find one that really smells good on me, I just go nuts with it. I had a hard time finding one that didn't turn into skunk smell when I applied it. Now I could cry, as both of the fragrances that had guys following me around sniffing and wanting more have been discontinued, and I can no longer purchase! Do you happen to know if there's a source for a Woodhue by Faberge? The other one is an Avon fragrance called "Cotillion" that could be purchased in an oil-based roll-on perfume. Only the oil-based one did the job. Thanks for a wonderful publication! I've learned a lot and truly love it!

Dear Carmen,

My ex-boyfriend wore Hugo Boss and Claiborne Sport. I loved both smells then, and I, too, am "reduced to a quivering mass" when anyone within a mile is wearing either one. It drove me so crazy for a while after we broke up (and even after I got a new boyfriend, yikes!) that I bought a little bottle of Hugo Boss to put on my pillow. Sweet dreams!

Dear Carmen,

I love your column! Thank you for keeping us all sexually aware with tastefulness. Most of the men I have dated since my separation and subsequent divorce do not wear fragrances or wear too much. I just wanted to comment that I have always been absolutely aroused by any man walking on the street with an old fragrance that some men still realize the sensual power of and wear the hell out of. No matter how a man looks, if he is wearing Aramis, I will follow him for as long as the wind sends the signal to my nose and further. It's almost like foreplay to me. I guess that this scent is also my fetish.

Today's Topic: Flirting

Remember how you first behaved when you met your partner? The subtle glance, hair twisting, and exchanging three-second glances? Yes, this is called flirting, and it suffers from neglect and bad press. Flirting is one of the first behaviors to die out in long-term relationships, and it's my duty to kick-start your perception of body language!

Back in the day (which day I don't know), flirting was once again associated with bad-girl behaviors and was thought to be the true indicator of cheap and tawdry sex. I'm not talking about the stereotypical gum-snapping, giggling, hair-flipping behavior, either. That should remain firmly entrenched in the hallways of junior high schools.

Flirting is actually considered so scientifically noteworthy that our friends in the clinical research department have narrowed down its fundamental purpose -- to get a mate. It all begins on a subconscious level, and there are over 52 basic moves women use as often as 70 or 80 times an hour. Women who were "high-signal" flirts attracted four times as many men than the "low-signalers" did.

It begins with a smile and evolves into a pout followed by the eyebrow flash, and finally eye contact. What amazes me is how many people are oblivious to the pupil dilation that happens when someone naturally finds someone attractive. This dilation allows more light to filter in so you can focus more clearly on your paramour. Once a woman engages in eye contact she'll begin rotating her head between 25 and 45 degrees, viewing the object of her affection from all angles.

The rest of it is automatic, and some women actually mimic bird behavior by exposing their necks while laughing at something. If you think I'm kidding, watch a group of women mingling at a bar and notice how many of them will stroke the front of their necks or play with their jewelry. Other behaviors include caressing any object on the table like the rim of a wine glass, cigarette lighter, pepper mill, cucumber...just kidding. After several minutes of the stroking behavior, they'll move into something more obvious like playing with their hair, smoothing their clothes, or the favorite skirt hike. Some are more brazen and run a lemon slice or a cherry across their lips. This enables women to expose their tongues (another borrowed trick from the animal kingdom) which most of my male friends go crazy over.

Crowded rooms are a great way to establish innocent body contact with a stranger. The most effective behavior is to linger in close contact before moving on. Most men will guide their way through a crowd by gently nudging the small of a woman's back, while most women will navigate a room by brushing into a man's forearm.

So, what's the point of this? It's all good! Don't stop making subtle contact with your partner just because you have been together for three years or more. Women in particular need to improve their flirting techniques because most men love this kind of attention. Let's face it, they are worth fussing over, so snap out of your funk and start batting those eyelashes!

♡ ♡ ♡ ♡ ♡ Reader Comments ♡ ♡ ♡ ♡ ♡

Hi,

Ladies, most of you out there are due an apology. Many of us men, and I hope yours is not one of them, have no idea what it takes to please their woman. They are simply there to enjoy the sex act for themselves. So they have no idea what they are missing by not making the attempt to take their woman into consideration. Foreplay and a slow hand are the key to making women explode. I seriously wonder how many men out there are even aware that foreplay can begin two or three days before the sex act. It can all begin with the simplest eye contact, then a handshake or touch, and then etc.etc.etc. So just a friendly word of advice to all the males who are reading this....slow down, make your mate enjoy the lovemaking, and you will be amazed at how much more you will enjoy that very same act. Thanks, Carmen. I love this media and just wanted to add my two cents worth. Please feel free to use it if you care to.

[I care, I care! Thanks.]

Dear Carmen,

I miss the days of flirting. A few years go I came across two men at a motel. We were all in the room for ice. I recognized them although I could only see the wonderful structure of their rear ends in skin tight jeans as they were bent over the machine. When they straightened with long blond hair flinging back, my heart pounded, and I knew I wanted the one. I had seen them on a stage (roadies). I decided to try something I had never done before. I played coy, and it covered many of your descriptions. After all, these were guys who were used to the other flirtations to outright aggression, and I wanted them all night. Acting coy worked, and we laughed about it later. I had done the "I am only a little female who has trouble with ths big bad machine and surely one of you gentlemen would help me." I can't believe I did that. I intend to do it more. I love your articles and look forward to more.

You go, Carmen.

There is nothing quite so subtly exciting as feeling a man's fingers in the small of your back, just in passing. Flirting is good, good, good. How simple a thing to remind us that we are desired and that our man is the object of our desire. A long look from across the room can heat evenings for weeks to come.

♡ ♡ ♡ ♡ ♡ ♡ ♡ ♡ ♡ ♡ ♡ ♡ ♡ ♡ ♡ ♡ ♡ ♡ ♡ ♡

Today's Topic: Kiss Me, Kiss Me, Kiss Me!

Since we've been discussing the basics, it's a good time to approach the all important starting point, the kiss. How this is handled can make or break a relationship, but some men downplay its importance.

See if this sounds familiar: you're about to surrender to a perfectly romantic moment. You and your partner are face to face with no doubt that a kiss is eminent so you close your eyes and...ick! You've either been slobbered, root-canaled, or gagged by the tongue that ate New Jersey. Perhaps a few tips about proper kissing would be in order to ensure a successful seduction. Trust me. Nothing brings a moment to a screeching halt faster than a bad kiss. My favorite horror story involves a man who thought that jamming his tongue across my upper gum-line was a real "Don Juan" technique...I never saw him again.

Few things are more powerful to a woman than a sensuous kiss. Whether the kiss is soft, lingering, warm, or brief, if it's done well, you'll melt her on the spot. You should learn how a woman wants to be kissed, but it really begins with feeling and intention. Give her the feeling that your next breath depends on kissing her and look out!

I'll start by reminding my gentlemen readers that slow and lingering is always better. Kevin Costner's rant in *Bull Durham* said it all, "...And I believe in slow, deep, soft, wet kisses that last for three days!" Oh my!

Women with full lips probably like to have their lower lip gently sucked into your mouth. Not all like it, so ask. Do not push your entire tongue into her mouth. Men have larger tongues than women and filling her entire mouth is not the object.

Find the proper tension for your lips while kissing. If your lips are too loose, the kiss will feel sloppy, and if they're too tight, she'll sense that you are nervous and not enjoying yourself.

Avoid quickly darting your tongue in and out of her mouth. It feels like an awkward simulation of woodpecker French kissing. Besides you don't want to make her laugh at this point, do you?

Try running the tip of your tongue on the inside of her lips before engaging the tip of her tongue. This lets her know you're planning on doing this for a while.

Kissing is important, so whatever you do, don't just go through the motions so you can pass go and collect your $200. She'll sense this and recoil. The kissing rule also follows the touching rule. You don't just touch her or kiss her as a prelude to sex only. If you only engage her as a means to an end, she'll feel like a pedestrian.

As a reminder to my married readers, sometimes you forget about the simple things. Take the time to renew your kissing technique. Remember, foreplay can start three days in advance. Let her know you're thinking about her and savoring the idea for days in advance. If you have any other sure-fire techniques, please share. I need your ideas. Happy kissing. :-)

 **Reader Comments**

Dear Carmen,

Men like to be kissed, too. All too often, when I kiss a woman, all she does is open her mouth. I suggest you tell your female readers that it takes two to kiss, and that she should put her tongue into his mouth. Or are you too much of a self-centered, man-hating sexist to do this?

[Sexist? Moi? Never! You stated your position quite clearly, so now my female readers will be reminded to return the kiss. Man hater? You're kidding right? I ADORE men; it's not just my job; its an adventure!]

Today's Topic: Drive Him Crazy Part I

In response to your mail, I've decided to devote the next three issues to indulging your man. That's right ladies, it's all about the guys this week. So choose the ideas you're comfortable with and remember that variety is the spice of life. So for God's sake, try something less ordinary and reap the rewards!

1. Wake him up by fondling his penis, morning or night.

2. See #1, only use your mouth.

3. Unzip or unbutton his pants and masturbate him while he's watching TV. Don't do this during the Superbowl while his friends are present.

4. Surprise him by sneaking into the shower while he's washing his hair and finish the job.

5. Cook breakfast or serve his coffee naked.

6. Phone him at work and talk dirty. Emails can be read, so use discretion.

7. Shave off all your pubic hair. Remember that the stubble can be a killer, so it's best to keep it clean once you've started this practice.

8. After dinner, dance in an erotic fashion. Polkas are not suggested.

9. Undress and take him to bed without saying a word. Sometimes talking is not necessary.

10. Videotape your lovemaking and watch it again on a rainy day.

11. Surprise him with naughty underwear if you're a flannel junkie.

12. Make his favorite dinner, but serve dessert on your skin.

13. Draw him a bath and wash him from head to toe, then make him return the gesture.

14. Watch an adult video while spooning...

15. Venture outside and have sex in your yard. However, first consider how close your neighbors are before trying this. (If they don't want to watch they can leave, right?)

16. Try the dominatrix persona by dressing in black leather, rubber, whips, and handcuffs. Turn on a rerun of "Father Knows Best" and see what happens when worlds collide.

17. Go to a club to see a great new band, but separate and seduce him from across the room like you've just met.

18. Eat at a romantic restaurant and during dinner take his hand under the table to demonstrate your lack of underwear.

19. Arrange to meet him at a hotel in the middle of the afternoon and have "an affair."

20. Make tonight a "no electricity" night. Use only candles and avoid the TV, which has killed many romantic evenings.

21. Shoot pool in high heels and a smile!

22. Buy him some sexy new underwear and insist on a fashion show.

This rather extensive list will be continued in the next edition of "Great Sexpectations."

♡ ♡ ♡ ♡ ♡ Reader Comments ♡ ♡ ♡ ♡ ♡

Hi, Carmen,

I don't know if this is exactly along the same lines, but my long distance love and I used a combination of the computer and the phone to have the most incredible sex ever. I was never more aroused. We talked for almost four hours focusing on each and every little detail, describing each act in detail, slowly touching. It is amazing how very erotic the mind can be.

[You sound very creative and enthused. Keep up the good work.]

Hi, Carmen,

Just the other day while making love with my boyfriend, he asked me to talk dirty to him. He had never asked me to do this before, so I was kind of surprised. I was a little uncomfortable about doing this, but tried uttering a few words anyway. Like I said, I was surprised as it has never been an issue before.

I love him very much, but how can I approach the subject sensitively with him that talking dirty does not do anything for me without it turning into some drama? I know communication is the key to a good relationship, but I really do not know how to approach him without offending him. I want to make him happy, but this is uncomfortable for me. Thank you for your help.

Dear Carmen,

Sending an email describing a desire or putting a note where it is sure to be found is always a pleasant surprise. Passionate kisses are always a plus. Not quick and hurried kisses, but kisses that take time and express your desires. (not necessarily a prelude to sex)

Today's Topic: More Ways to Drive Him Crazy

If you're just tuning in, this edition is the second installment of a three-part series about pleasing your man. Before I continue with this list, I need to reiterate that these ideas aren't comfortable for everyone, so pick and choose the ones you feel most comfortable with.

Please understand that some of the greatest coupling takes place between two trusting and willing partners with a sense of confidence, whimsy, and HUMOR! Don't be afraid to fuse humor with sex. They can be a great combination.

These suggestions work on the principle of surprise. The reason I'm supplying a list is so you can spice up the mundane routine you've fallen into. The biggest complaint I get is from men and women who are bored with the same old pattern. You were adventurous when you first started dating so...

1. Mow the lawn in a sexy outfit and make sure he's there to see it!

2. Take him on a picnic to a secluded location and wear something with easy access.

3. Allow him to explore your entire body, including your anus, if he has expressed curiosity.

4. Hold his penis while he urinates.

5. Assume a new sexual identity: the naughty librarian, the pissed-off postal worker, or try a whorish Pippy Longstocking just for grins.

6. Give him a full-body massage and take at least an hour. The more time you spend on him, the better it gets.

7. Change the oil in the car without being told first. (Foreplay has many identities.)

8. Listen to Yanni. He'll be so annoyed he'll do anything to make it stop!

9. Try really listening to him. It's a shame when people who love each other stop making their mate the first priority.

10. Describe a sexual fantasy to him in detail, then ask to try it out.

11. Kiss him without letting him kiss you back. You're in charge now.

12. Buy sex toys from a catalog together, no kidding.

13. In the middle of the night, light a candle and run your fingers through his hair until he wakes up.

14. Have him invite his friends over for an all-night poker game. Make the snacks and wait on them hand and foot. No, it's not very sexy, but hey, this is for the guys, right?

15. Rent an action film and watch it with him in one of his flannel shirts, socks, and no underwear.

16. Feed him in bed. I don't care what it is, anything edible will do.

17. Ask him how to perfect your oral sex techniques. It will be the most descriptive and clear conversation you've ever had. If he wants to provide you with sketches, get the pencil!

18. Listen to a CD that you heard on your first date. If there was no music, then hum.

19. Humming? See #17.

20. Pack his lunch and throw some nude Polaroids of yourself in the bag. If you really want to surprise him, throw in the nude Polaroids you took of him while he was sleeping...SURPRISE, HONEY!

I know what you're thinking: Carmen, I thought these were supposed to be serious and helpful. Guess what? They are! You are only limited by your imagination, so if you think a towel fight would be fun, commence snapping. It's all about the effort you want to make for your relationship, so it's all good!

 ## Reader Comments

Dear Carmen,

I agree, humor's the key. Just as women can do the finger-to-palm thing to figure a man's size, men,--did you know that you could judge the size of a woman's breasts by staring intently at them? Also helpful in judging the power of her right jab!

[I loved this letter!]

Dear Carmen,

I just wanted to let you know about a fun idea that I tried with my boyfriend: I French kissed him with Pop Rocks in my mouth. To say the least, he was very suprised. In case you do not know what they are, Pop Rocks are a fruit candy proccessed with carbon dioxide. The latter makes them tingle and fizz as soon as they come into contact with moisture. My boyfriend said the sensation of the fizzing in his mouth was a turn on.

Would this be safe to try with oral sex? I am not sure if I should try it with oral sex, so could you please reply back to me? Thanks

Today's Topic: Male Erogenous Zones

I was having a discussion yesterday with some of my colleagues over making some managerial changes that would simplify a project. It was a typical meeting, and near the end of it somebody uttered their prediction, "You know, we can lead the horse to water, but we can't make him drink." Knowing that my mind is never far from this column, I realized that he was right! Like the horse, I lead my readers to the erogenous zones, but I didn't make any suggestions about what to do with them! Silly me. Perhaps a few suggestions would be in order.

Around Valentine's Day I supplied a list of erogenous zones as if it should be treated as a check list. It occurred to me that not everyone shares the same skills when dealing with each area, so why not make a few rules about what to try and what to avoid? Most people associate erogenous zones with places to kiss or caress, but it's not always so cut and dry.

Let's start with the male erogenous zones. These zones are not supposed to be methodically played within a certain order like some ritual behavior. My biggest pet peeve involves people who treat foreplay like a recipe: kiss ears twice, caress nipples once, and open the safe...wrong! It's crucial that you always change directions and try to avoid doing things the same way. Erogenous zones act like receptors for more passionate behavior, but you must tease and skim the surface, or it just becomes overkill.

1. Ears - This is always a successful yet natural point to begin. Why you ask? Because conversation is always the best way to initiate closer contact. Try lowering the volume enough to necessitate closer proximity. Rather than starting with kisses to the ear, whisper close enough to almost brush your lips against his ear, but stop short of contact and allow him to feel your warm breath against his ear. After you

feel the small pocket of warmth, then brush the tip of your nose against his ear while gently kissing his neck.

2. Lips - I know what you're thinking, "Duh! Kissing is always a great way to initiate intimacy, so tell us something we don't know!" It's not always about being lip to lip. Try tracing the fullest part of his mouth with the tip of your finger or your nose. Try whispering while you guide his eyelids shut with your lips as well.

3. Nipples - I'm always surprised at the amount of women who don't know about male nipple sensitivity. You can make small circles around the nipples with everything from your tongue to a small feather. Because they are sensitive, don't twist or pull. Don't concentrate for too long, or you'll diminish the effect.

4. Armpits - This is frequently overlooked so before you forget, try running the back of your finger tips along the curvature of his armpit. Again, you do not always have to approach these zones with your lips. This area can be slightly tricky because some people are so incredibly ticklish that you'll break the mood by inducing spastic aversion retaliation which usually ends in hysterical laughing rather than...well...you know, right?

5. Buttocks - Hugely overlooked! This is one of those areas that gets an immediate response from most men. I'm not suggesting that you just grab a handful and squeeze, either. Try to work your way down by massaging his back muscles. If he's laying over your lap, incorporate the same kneading technique you would use if you were making bread. I could throw in a "rising" joke, but that would be too obvious.

6. Genitalia - This goes without saying, but rather than just going for broke, it's important to spend time in the general vicinity. Depending on what the situation calls for, use your lips or your hands and try one

of the non-response activities. For those of you who missed it, the non-response activity requires that he simply closes his eyes and just concentrates on the sensations you provide. Verbalize what feels good and don't approach it with any expectations. Remember the more relaxed you are and the slower you go, the more enhanced your experience will be.

7. Feet - Please establish the tickle factor with your partner! Some people have violently ticklish feet, so avoid this if your partner is one of them. If it's okay, proceed to rub the bottom of his feet in small circular motions. Use a firmer grip on the feet than other areas because if you handle them too lightly, you'll wind up in tickle land again.

As I stated earlier, these erogenous zones contain nerve endings that can easily heighten physical activity. I'm not suggesting that you ignore other parts of the body during foreplay, just incorporate this into more of your plan. Playing with hair, running a fingertip across your partner's cheek, and other small gestures create a relaxed atmosphere with enough potential passion to light up a small city. Next issue we'll cover the female erogenous zones, but until next time, explore, enjoy, and always use your powers for good--never evil!

♡ ♡ ♡ ♡ ♡ **Reader Comments** ♡ ♡ ♡ ♡ ♡

Dear Carmen,

I can't believe I am writing this, but here it goes. I am in a wonderful relationship with an unbelievable man. Our sex life is good and could use improvement as with any new (five months) relationship. My question and concern is: I want to explore him from his head to his toes with my mouth, fingers, hands, etc., but when I try, he can't handle it. He is so ticklish and maybe self-conscious or uncomfortable, I am not sure which, that it distracts me, turns me off, and makes me self-conscious of what I am doing. I love this man deeply and want to know every part of him and please him in every way. How can I do this if I cannot get him to relax, be less self-conscious, or less sensitive? Since I don't know the real deal, I can't say. When I ask him, he says he's ticklish. I also notice he doesn't ever get an erection, so I guess it doesn't turn him on. Please answer. I am not sure what is the next step. I have gone to Fredericks of Hollywood and got a blindfold. I haven't used it yet. Is that a good start?

[It's a fine start. Keep going until you find something you agree with.]

Dear Carmen,

I am in a relationship with a woman who insists that there is something rather odd that my nipples don't provide me pleasure. As a 38-year-old male, I really never considered if they were supposed to or not. Now I'm curious, are they supposed to?

[Some men have lots of nerve endings; others do not. You're perfectly normal.]

Dear Carmen,

You were talking about good places to touch a man, and another good place to touch is his inner thighs. Below his balls is also another one. If you massage lightly, it's a great sensation from him. Also the inner works of his hands make him relaxed. If you gently kiss it, he is more aroused. He also likes the back of his neck kissed and even the lower of the back and waist. When those two spots are kissed and gently caressed, it can send feelings and emotions flying! Both partners like that. Enjoy the tips!

Thanks for listening. These were just some more ideas.

Today's Topic: Female Erogenous Zones

Last time we covered the male erogenous zones and how to incorporate them into your intimacy routine. This time we'll discuss the female erogenous zones and list a few suggestions that will give you her undivided attention.

Before we work our way down the list of female sweet spots, I should qualify something I said last time about erogenous zones and foreplay. At no time did I mean that you should only engage these zones for the purposes of foreplay. As a matter of practice, you should familiarize yourself with these spots to keep things interesting. Every once in a while it's a great idea to just tantalize for the sake of pleasure and not as a preview to sex. The whole idea is to keep your relationship unpredictable. When things become routine, interests start to wax and wane. Wax is bad enough, but waning? Really bad.

Anyhoo, for those taking notes, let's start with the female erogenous zones and talk about what works best.

1. Neck - Not just any part of the neck, but the BACK of the neck. Starting in the hollow part behind her ear, try to just barely brush the surface of her skin with your breath before initiating light contact. The goal is to try to keep the touch light enough to be noticed, but not so light that it starts to tickle. Kissing is always a plus, but remember to measure her state of euphoria based on how deep she is breathing.

2. Breasts - I know it's another obvious zone, but try to avoid going immediately to the nipples. The whole breast area is sensitive from the bottom of the neck, so start nibbling or touching her collar bone. Start by making small circles and gradually spread them out until you cup your hand gently under her breasts. The nipples should be your eventual destination, not the first.

3. Ribs - Not the entire rib cage, but the area closer to the breasts. Press gently and follow the lines of her ribs toward her breasts, but stop short of her actual breasts. You can use your tongue, fingers, or even the tip of your nose. If you want to add a little spice, try the tip of a feather or a Q-tip! Use your imagination (I know you've got one).

4. Navel - This is another one of those love/hate zones. Find out if this tickles her fancy before you try it. If she's into it, use anything from your tongue to a strawberry. Don't make me explain the fruit...

5. Inner thighs - It sounds obvious, but don't just use her thighs as an expressway to her genitals. Spend some serious time caressing the inside of her legs and tease her by stopping just short of the mark. The thighs are one of your best choices for massage oils or lotions.

6. Back of the knees - Women know enough to put perfume back here so make sure you take the time to notice. It's also a very ticklish spot for some, so you would do better to kiss her gently and work your way to the inside of her thighs.

7. Toes - I hear toe sucking goes over big for some, but I was amazed to find out how many haven't tried this. I guess it goes without saying that practicing good hygiene is crucial before trying this. If you want to start slow, caress her toes while giving her a foot massage and work between. I don't know any woman who would turn down a foot massage, so your chances of playing footsie look pretty good.

Again, these erogenous zones are the established ones, but it doesn't mean that all women want attention in all these spots. If you've made a resolution to keep communications clear, start by establishing where she likes to be touched. She's not sure which zones are her favorite? I guess you'll have to go on a little fact-finding mission. I don't really see any down side here, do you?

♡ ♡ ♡ ♡ ♡ Reader Comments ♡ ♡ ♡ ♡ ♡

Dear Carmen,

I love your newsletter. I had to tell you that the first time a guy sucked my toes, I thought, WOW, that's my toe, and if it feels like that on my toe, I can see why a guy likes a blow job so much. I don't mind doing it for him so much now. So try it, guys! You might get more in return!

Dear Carmen,

I love your column. It is very helpful. I was wondering if you will write anything about breast sensitivity? My wife claims hers are not sensitive, but during sex she likes to have the nipples squeezed. I'm not sure what to do. Can you address this topic? Thanks.

[My doctor refers to this as "numb nipples." Some women have fewer nerve endings. Some become numb after breast augmentation. She might want to consult her doctor if it's a concern. I am not an MD.]

Dear Carmen,

I believe a woman needs loving and time, a trailing kiss that goes from the cheek down the neck with a few nibbles here and there. To hold and snuggle your woman is very important to a healthy love life. Foreplay should last all day, 24/7 and every now and then a break to leave it open that when her man touches her, she will expect it to last for awhile and relax and open like a flower. To make her cum in seconds is a trick that has it's drawbacks, but the silk tongue keeps her cumming back for more. You as the man must take time to learn her orgasmic body. Then a kiss is not just a kiss :-)~

I learned what I know and must give credit where credit is due, to a lesbian couple that agreed to teach me how to please a woman.

Today's Topic: The Urethral Sponge

I will continue to sympathize with my male readers over the mystery that is the female body. While you think you have a handle on what makes her purr, there's always a question about what you think she likes and what she really likes. One of the ground rules for women is that no two are alike, so there is no magic formula for all women.

The urethral opening is located between the clitoris and the vagina and is usually associated with urination. What makes this area worth consideration is its close proximity to the vagina and the G-Spot. This whole area is filled with a spongy erectile tissue containing paraurethral glands and ducts. This spongy tissue becomes engorged during stimulation, but not all women find it remarkable. On the other hand, some women find it highly arousing and desire this area to be stimulated during intercourse. If you're interested in finding it, the best method is to approach it by pressing through the front wall of the vagina. This spongy area can fill with fluid that some women ejaculate during sex.

If you're new to the column, I've had previous discussions about female ejaculation and the G-Spot. What I find troubling is the amount of mail I receive from readers that worry about the whys and the why-nots of certain behaviors. If you're a woman who can't experience a vaginal orgasm without clitoral stimulation, you're perfectly normal. If you're a man who worries that his partner doesn't have female ejaculation, that too is perfectly normal. Not all women are physically capable of the same experiences, but what you have to remember is that sexual endeavors change from woman to woman. Look at it like all women have one area of sexuality at which they excel. Your only concern should be that you have a mutually satisfying experience with each other, and don't be so worried about outcome. It doesn't take a genius to know if you're sexually compatible with someone or not, but it does take patience and communication to see if you can improve your relations. Take the urethral sponge for instance. You might be dating somebody who doesn't even know that this area is stimulating because nobody ever tried, or you might be with somebody who knows about it, but prefers to have her nipples kissed instead. Yes, female genitalia is all internal, but don't be discouraged from experimenting.

Moving along to what some of my male readers call the female "taint." The proper word for this erogenous area is the perineum. This is the area between the vaginal opening and the anus. If you go between the back wall of the vagina and the rectum, there is a similar spongy body of tissue called the perineal sponge which can also be highly arousing. This area is close to the muscles of the pelvic floor and is connected to the pudendal nerve, which is the primary pathway of stimulation to the clitoris.

Due to the large amount of nerve endings and the proximity to the vagina, this area is also hugely arousing to women. More than likely, the women who enjoy having the perineal sponge stimulated probably appreciate anal stimulation as well, but it is always in your best interest to ask first.

I get several e-mails every week from women who are worried when their partners ask them if they'll try anal sex. Don't get the perineal sponge mixed up with anal sex. They're two separate activities. If you're worried about it, perhaps your partner would be willing to stimulate just the outside of your rectal area to see how you react.

I have no sage wisdom to share about this--only that some women LOVE this and others hate it. Some fall in the middle of the scale so while they don't particularly enjoy it, they don't dislike it either. Many in this category will engage because their partner has shown an interest. Again, it's a personal choice, and I can't give you a magic test or indicator that never fails. I've been friends with women who found anal stimulation perfectly erotic with one partner and totally out of the question with others.

I'm just giving some more anatomy tips for you to play with. I neither condemn nor condone. Like Jack Webb said, "Just the facts, ma'am."

Reader Comments

Carmen:

Some men refer to the perineum (taint) as a chin rest because it serves just that function.

Dear Carmen,

I have been reading you for a while now. While I find your e-mails to be absolutely fantastic and am willing to try all aspects, I find that my boyfriend, although interested, is too lazy to do or try anything. While he agrees you are right on the mark, he does nothing! In past relationships I have found men to be of the same mind. They would rather the girlfriend be the one to make moves and changes if any are to be made. What they complain about most of the time after being with a mate or partner for a long period of time is that women lose sexual interest! This is not always true.

Trust me, if men would put more into the foreplay of the sexual relationship, we females would never lose interest. As a matter of fact, we would be a lot more sexually oriented, at least from my experience. Thanks for all your e-mails.

[You're welcome! Everyone reaps what they sow, especially with sex.]

Today's Topic: Minding the Stepchildren

Today we need to address the often overlooked yet sensitive world of male testicles. It's no surprise that most of your letters continue to ask about oral sex, but I need to remind everyone that it's more than just direct contact with the penis that makes for more enticing sex. If you find yourself wondering how to make your sessions more exotic, there are several areas worth consideration.

Many women avoid the perineum which is the soft, hairless skin between the testicles and the anus. With carefully-manicured fingers, stroke this area with your free hand in a "come over here" motion. After he becomes used to this (which won't take long), stroke his testicles in the same manner. I need to stress how sensitive his testicles are so as a guide, you should always handle them with the same amount of pressure you would use while handling small fragile eggs. His balls have many nerve endings which means you can go from pleasure to pain very fast. The balls or "stepchildren" are often overlooked during sex because some women are afraid of hurting their partners. One technique you can try involves moving your tongue around his balls until you very gently take one in your mouth at a time while caressing him with your tongue in small circles.

With your free hand roam around his body by lightly scratching his inner thighs. Because your skin is the largest organ on your body you need to constantly touch EVERYWHERE, not just the genitals! Make sure you balance your stroking. If you massage one part of his body, remember to contact both sides of his body in the same spot, i.e. inner right thigh and inner left thigh. Most of us are keenly aware when the stroking becomes erratic and contained in one small area, so roam freely. Try teasing his pubic hair softly while caressing his stepchildren. Try not to linger while you're trying this because it's important to engage his whole body. Run your finger down from his bellybutton to his pubic bone while taking a break from oral stimulation. Teasing in small steps will quickly build the anticipation instead of feeling like you're on a military mission. Passion can quickly turn to aerobics if you're not careful with your timing, so if you are wondering how to judge your progress, simply listen to his breathing. The deeper and more intense his breathing becomes, the more involved he is in what you're doing.

Let's review the most important words used today; gently, lightly, stroking, and caressing cannot be stressed enough when you're engaging his perineum or testicles. These are intensely sensitive so you should approach with deference and skill. If you're afraid of hurting him, ask your partner to talk you through it. He should be more than willing to share how this feels by letting you know exactly how much pressure to exert. No two men are identical, so some prefer almost no pressure while others can handle intense amounts of stroking, sucking, and licking. Exploring is half of the fun, so relax and enjoy everything! The stepchildren method is also referred to as "tea-bagging" which always makes me think of honey.

 **Reader Comments**

Dear Carmen,

Now this article is really damn good. I have to try this; it sounds like too much fun! Thanks for the suggestion! - A loyal reader

♀ Chapter Four ♂

Mind, Body, and Soul

Eastern wisdom does not mean "go paak the caar." While I would never insult my brethren in Boston, I'm talking about something even further East and something that transcends time. Sensate practices involve the mind before the body and teach us how to fully experience the most from our intimate encounters from breathing to exchanging sexual energies. Once you learn these techniques, you'll really understand the expression "you reap what you sow." Sensate practices start at ground zero in terms of really learning your own breathing as well as your partner's. Without sounding too "out there," it's really the closest thing to sexual meditation that I've learned. Sensate practices go beyond researching your sexual urges; they ask you to incorporate your whole body, mind, and soul in the experience.

So far I have heard nothing but fantastic reviews from my subscribers who have tried this. It is not just because it feels great. As they practice sensate, they begin to share a new bond with their partner which has taken their relationship to a whole new level of intimacy. You will notice as you read the book that there is a definite theme behind each column, which is to incorporate great sex into your lifestyle without treating it as a separate event.

This isn't for the wishy-washy, either. You must commit to the idea that you want to experience your sexual relationship actively and at all levels. So, does this sound interesting?

Today's Topic: Anticipation

I watched an ad on TV the other night that brought high school back in a flood of memories. Two girls were talking on the phone (the true hallmark of teenhood) about a first kiss. The one giggled that she hadn't tried yet, but it would probably be soon. It was the anticipation that made these years so exciting, and at the same time I started thinking about my first kiss (with a mouth full of braces). I also wondered what happened to the guy who gave me my first kiss and wondered what his recollection of the event would be if I happened to run into him.

Please indulge my little stroll down memory lane before I jump into today's topic. So back to the first kiss. I'm 15, and a SENIOR took me to my first Chicago White Sox game. I don't remember anything about the night except being too nervous to eat my pizza and worrying about the kiss goodnight at the DOOR! My date was the most sought after co-captain of the football team, and I was terrified. The end of the night brought the longest walk I've ever endured. Of course I handled myself with coolness and decorum. I closed my eyes and turned my cheek into his approaching lips. It was the abject fear of cold orthodontic metal marring his perfect lips that sent me into flight mode. I guess a peck on the cheek was not the frenzied passion he was used to, and we never went out again, but isn't it funny how we can remember this stuff like it happened last night?

Anticipation plays a huge part in our romantic endeavors from our teen years through adulthood. If I had to break down the old saying that absence makes the heart grow fonder, I'd have to say that it's the anticipation of the reunion that makes us really crazy, right? At this moment my significant other is working out of town for a week, but the idea of what will happen when he gets back is what raises my blood pressure. Couples who have been together for a while forget how to anticipate their time together, and one of the arguments I get revolves around no more surprises. "Carmen, we know each other too well for this kind on nonsense." Bull. If you keep experiencing new ideas, hobbies, sexual practices, and the occasional best seller, you'll keep discovering new things about each other. Remember my biggest pet peeve about people who live on automatic pilot? Don't do it!

♡ ♡ ♡ ♡ ♡ Reader Comments ♡ ♡ ♡ ♡ ♡

Hi, Carmen,

What do you make of a man's comment that he doesn't know which arouses him more, the sight of my breasts or the sight of my buttocks? He is a highly sensual man.

[Yes, he is. You're lucky to be so fully appreciated. Hang on to him!]

Hey, Carmen,

I just wanted to let you know that you're right, and not everyone in the world manages to lose that anticipation. My boyfriend is in the Air Force right now, though he won't always be, but that's beside the point. Every time we're apart, even for a few hours, I can't help but miss him, and I look forward to seeing him again. We spent three months apart this last Spring, and almost no one could understand why I was so anxious to see him again. The only people who did understand had been in my same spot.

When we got together again, well, let's just say that we spent a week catching up. I've got to say that there are advantages to the military life because while you miss your significant other unbearably when he's gone, you can't help but look forward to when he will come back and the time immediately following his return.

Today's Topic: Sensate Focus

At the risk of sounding like a broken record, you can't separate the mind from the body. One of the first mistakes we make in terms of sexual philosophy entails feeling with the body first, with the mind running a close second. Wrong. To illustrate further I'd like to allude to the most common experience women share. It all starts as a promising night. You're relaxed, you've had a wonderful evening, and the impending romance is going great. Foreplay was satisfying, and you're aching to take it to the next level when suddenly the mood takes a radical turn.

While you were riding the wave of natural progression and reading one another like soul mates, he starts to drill like a jackhammer. Rather than feeling excited, you're totally distracted from the moment because your head is suffering through a speed bag pummeling from the headboard. Oooooooh yeaaaaah ummmmmmmmm OUCH, OUCH, OUCH! Let's be honest. The mood is broken.

Wait! I'm not ripping on the wonderful male species; I'm simply explaining that men can get very intense in a short period of time. By the way, they're following their instincts, which is right. The only amendment you should strive for is time and more of it. One of the most frustrating aspects of sex is that we all want it to last longer, right? Who wants something that great to end quickly?

Enter sensate focus exercises. In the spirit of "know thyself," you should begin by sensitizing yourself to your own arousal process. Treat your body like an instrument and learn to fine tune your craft. Remember that the point of sensate focus is not arousal or orgasm. Your only task is to appreciate the sensations during the exercises.

This technique is perfect for the couple experiencing boredom due to routine and lack of passion. There are only three rules to remember.

1. Pay close attention to where you are being touched and what you're touching. Stay as focused as possible.

2. Stay centered only on the physical sensations. Avoid spacing out or stressing over what happened at work. Be here and now only.

3. Whether you're alone or with your partner, enter these exercises without an agenda. In other words, stop expecting and simply experience the touching without any pressure. No demands mean you can escape judging the moment. Treat it like breathing. You know you're breathing, so pay attention to the air passing through your system.

Keeping these rules in mind, you should also choose a room that is conducive to intimacy. Stay away from phones, pagers, televisions, or rabid animals. I suggest trying silence instead of music. I know, that may sound wrong, but I promise, it is not. You're trying to achieve total focus not foreplay. Keep a water-based lubricant and a towel near for your first exercise.

Because this is an exercise, you should start by assigning roles. One partner will have the passive role, and the other has the active role. Because you are learning how to lightly caress your partner's genitals, you have to stay focused on the experience instead of shifting your attention from sensate focus to foreplay. How can you tell the difference? This is easy. Have you ever kissed a friend you've known forever only to stop suddenly because something was "different?" Intuition is a powerful force, and non-verbal communication is the easiest to detect, so stick with the program!

On Monday we'll discuss what each partner should practice, so set aside an hour and a half--five minutes to read me, and the rest for sensate focus. Until then, slow down and concentrate.

♡ ♡ ♡ ♡ ♡ Reader Comments ♡ ♡ ♡ ♡ ♡

Dear Carmen,

This was worse than a soap opera. You got me all excited about what is going to happen on Monday. Shish, do I have to wait until then to start? Hehehe. Not patiently yours, XXX

Today's Topic: Sensate Practices

First decide who will have the active role and who will have the passive role. For the sake of argument, let's say that the woman has decided to take the passive role. She must lie on her back and take enough time to be totally relaxed. Some take a long time, and some will just have to find out for the first time (you'd be amazed at the amount of people who have trouble relaxing).

After she's TOTALLY relaxed and not even a minute before, slowly and gently stroke the front of her body for at least 20 minutes. This caress should be done very slowly, giving her time to experience how your hand feels as it runs across her skin. The caress should focus on her genital area; however, it is not limited to only her genitals. Try to choose a center of gravity in your circle and concentrate on touching her as lightly as possible. It's usually at this point where couples are prone to cheat by changing the intention of the exercise. Resist temptation, please. You will not regret it.

After you've adjusted to the outside of her body, slowly use your fingers or tongue to stroke the outside and inside of her vagina. Do not plunge inside of her opening. Start by separating her labia away from her clitoral bud. If you're using your fingers, use lots of lubrication. Close your eyes and concentrate on how her body feels. Imprint on her skin texture, scent, and reaction (her physical response or change with your touch). She should only breathe deeply; if she's moaning, you've lost the focus of the exercise and have to start over. Her job is to experience your touch, not react. If she starts to tense up, give her a gentle reassuring pat on the thigh encouraging her to relax. Don't let your mind stray from what you're doing. If you start to drift, refocus on the experience. The only goal here is to achieve pleasure. Center on the pleasure you feel while touching her, and she should center on the sensations you deliver to her.

After 45 minutes or so, it's time to switch. Now the man has the passive role, and the woman has the active role. The man should lie down with his legs slightly spread and keep his arms relaxed on his sides. He should remain in the same position for the duration of your caressing. Using plenty of lubricant, slide your hands or mouth around his genitals concentrating on how his penis and scrotum feels. A relaxed penis feels just as sensual as an erect penis; it's just in a different way.

Concentrate on the different textures from the head, to the rim, to his testicles. Most men find it difficult to not become erect, so this is really not a problem. Even though arousal is not the focus, you can still certainly appreciate how his body responds to your fingers. He should not flex or move his PC muscle during this. He is not expected to "do" anything with his erection except feel it. If you feel him starting to tense up, try to refocus his attention. Passive or active, both of you should be concentrating on only one thing: the sensations you're sharing. If you're uncomfortable doing this with a partner, you can also try it on your own. No, it's not a masturbation exercise. It's intended to be a fact-finding mission about your body.

During this caress session, take notice of the areas of your body that have more nerve endings or less sensations. Did you find a little spot where you were extremely sensitive? Did you prefer some of the touching to be lighter or heavier in some areas? What about your partner? How did their genitals feel in your hands? After trying this a few times, you'll notice that the increased focus changes the way you touch each other. More importantly, it will change the way you perceive being touched. This exercise will help you center on your body which will bring us to the next level: more aware and more aroused. Next time we'll discuss what to do with this new level of sensual experience. Now relax and caress your partner! That's a firm request, not an order.

Reader Comments

Carmen,

I am in a new relationship and am having a hard time staying focused during sex, and I feel like I am building towards an orgasm, then without warning I am thinking about things that may have happened during the day or shopping or anything. This is making it hard to have an orgasm without having to use a vibrator. With my former partner of 18 years, I hardly ever used a vibrator to have an orgasm.

It is not that I mind using a vibrator, and my boyfriend doesn't mind either. I would just like to have an orgasm through his touch. I have used a vibrator for the last two to three years (once or twice a month) due to not being in a relationship. Has using a vibrator for awhile caused me to be dependent on the vibrator? Do you have any suggestions on relaxing and staying focused? Thanks for your help!

[Try the sensate focus exercise in a dim room with no music, no distractions, and no expectations. If you concentrate on your sensations you should be able to block out the day.]

Today's Topic: Non-Responsive Touching

It might be a Spring thing in the air, but lately I've been receiving e-mail from readers who feel anxious over the lack of responsiveness they feel from their partners. A while back I suggested a non-responsive exercise, but I think in retrospect I should have called it something else. The whole word "exercise" has a must do or obligatory ring to it. I think in order to get in touch with your partner, the boundaries need to be more clearly defined.

Some of my readers are writing out of frustration which is perfectly understandable, but some are writing for help because they're young and not sure about what makes their partner feel good. This practice should help you get through any of these awkward phases.

Younger couples are sometimes stressed because they think that everything just magically happens like in a movie. You kiss, it gets hot and heavy, and suddenly you're five steps ahead of where your body really is. Slowing things down is always a great suggestion, but if you don't address the questions, you'll end up back in the awkward zone again.

It's unfortunate, but not everybody knows their body and how it responds to stimulation. I hear some women/men saying that they feel obliged to get sexually stimulated as soon as they're touched, which is not the case. Both partners feel a certain amount of pressure, but the irony is that it only gets good when the pressure is off. The whole idea behind non-responsive touching is its simplicity. Your only directive is to feel. I promise--that's it.

One partner lies in a comfortable, dimly-lit room partially dressed or totally naked. The degree of dressing is up to the person. You must agree to play by the rules which only means that one person is the toucher, and the other person is the touchee. The real genius behind this is the simplicity. The toucher very silently runs their finger tips over their partner, and I mean everywhere. Start near an earlobe or the neck, but the key is to go slowly. As you're touching your partner (without conversation), close your eyes and just concentrate on how it feels. If you're thinking about how you're feeling, you'll suddenly become aware of which spots tickle your fancy more than others. This is the perfect time to understand where your personal hot spots are. Now, I'm not saying that this doesn't lead to arousal because it probably does. It's important that you treat it as a fact-finding mission and not a seduction.

Continue touching your partner all over and work your hand around every inch of his/her body. Lightly caress the genitals, abdomen, thighs, knees, and then turn over and work the back. You would be amazed at how many people were never given the time to understand their own sensations. Not everybody feels comfortable masturbating, and for those who are, it's about the whole body, not just the genitals. Non-responsive means you have no obligation to perform, reciprocate, retaliate, or initiate sex. The whole idea is to understand your sensations with your partner and to introduce sensuality to your whole body.

After 45 minutes or so, it's time to switch roles. The toucher now becomes the touchee, and you must hold to the agreement that you'll just lay still and enjoy. The tough part is keeping it from escalating into something more passionate, but the whole idea is to give yourself time and try to understand your body. Not everybody quivers like Jell-O over the same things, and the problems begin when you rush to get to a certain level of intimacy.

It's not wrong that you want to experience this with your partner; it's wrong that you don't take the time to figure out what works for you two. You must adjust to the situation, the person, their feelings, likes, and dislikes. Just because something worked with your last partner doesn't mean it's a done deal with your new one. I think the most common mistake is trying to handle your partner's needs before you know your own.

If you both take the time to study your bodies, I guarantee that you'll both be working with a new knowledge base, and everything just gets better. To the readers who tell me that they have trouble having an orgasm, I can say that this will put you in touch with what's missing, which is usually comfort. If you aren't totally relaxed, your body will never let go. Try this and please tell me how different your lovemaking feels. I'll expect lots of mail, but before you start, make sure your nails are smooth. There's nothing more painful than a ragged nail, especially down there! I wish you luck and much touching!

♡ ♡ ♡ ♡ ♡ Reader Comments ♡ ♡ ♡ ♡ ♡

Dear Carmen,

This is an interesting move for those who need to learn new forms of pleasure. I commend thee greatly! However, the same erotic pleasures can be examined with a full body massage. If you know what you're doing, it can bring about moments of pleasurable sensations to scramble your brain. If you don't believe this, let me massage you.

[My readers are such givers! Bless your heart!]

Hi, Carmen,

I've been doing this technique for years with my partner, and there is no doubt, this works and works in more ways than one. As I like to express it, it can be as good as the best sex and parallel with the wildest rollercoaster! Candles, music, temperature, and lighting help also!

Today's Topic: Exchanging Sexual Energy

If you've ever heard the expression "take my breath away," it might sound like a bad line from a cheesy romance novel, but it's actually rooted in the ancient practice of soul mating. The exchange and transfer of breathing between partners dates back to our friends the Taoists and their study of sexual transcendence. If you can't remember the last time someone took your breath away, keep reading.

What is it about sexuality that most of us find so intriguing? Besides the obvious physical pleasure, it really has more to do with transcending your usual physical boundaries. Lovemaking allows us to transcend our bodies by fusing with another human being. Most people experience this kind of transcendence in their bedrooms more than they do in churches, synagogues, or mosques. It is through sexual union that one can align himself with the rest of the universe, and it's my job to outline how to perform soul mating. As usual, this practice is only successful between deeply connected couples.

1. Expanding - This is the first stage that takes place during intercourse. When a woman becomes highly excited, she naturally increases lubrication or her yin energy. It is at this point where both partners can circulate this sexual energy through their bodies' own Microcosmic Orbits.

2. Gazing - After you're both engaged in exchanging your yin and yang energy (female and male energy), embrace your partner in a face-to-face position. Depending on the weight of the female, she should be on top in a sitting position. Look deeply into each other's eyes and send both love and energy to each other.

3. Breathing - Coordinating your breathing is essential for the exchange of chi, and gentlemen you must remember it is crucial to

gauge her breathing during foreplay. Once a woman is relaxed and ready, it is her breathing that becomes deeper, which is your signal to commence. Don't just check to see how damp she's getting, it's her breathing you should pay more attention to. Try to place your nose near her ear and your ear near her nose so you can both coincide your breathing until you reach a definitive rhythm.

4. Circulating - At this point you must both direct your energy in an orbit which runs up the back of your spine and down the midline of your body. You can draw this energy in a circle by using your mind and contracting your PC muscles while guiding the energy down the front of your body with your tongues.

The next time you see someone sporting a yin/yang tattoo ask yourself, "Does this person actually practice this, or is he or she just making a fashion statement?" For those in the know, sex is far beyond fashion or posturing, and it's my duty to separate the frauds from the enlightened. Keep breathing!

 Reader Comments

Dear Carmen,

There's a lot more to the yin/yang thing than this exchange of sexual energy. 'Tis true that most Americans who wear the symbol sense the "coolness" of it, but don't truly grasp the hugeness of the yin/yang concept. Yin/yang pertains to all things, physical, emotional, and spiritual.

♀ Chapter Five ♂

The Feminine Mystique

Women have incredible capabilities, but many are never engaged in the manner to which great things could happen. The challenge about being a woman surrounds the mysteries of her body. For centuries men have been baffled by female sexuality, primarily because her genitals are interior and not obvious to the naked eye. The G-Spot as well as other phenomenon like female ejaculation are rarely taught in school. If they had been, I'll bet you wouldn't have slept through your health class! I can say that most of my mail still comes from both men and women who fret over the almighty vaginal orgasm. I'm daunted by the amount of people who are troubled by this. The typical letter usually concerns the situation where the woman experiences the clitoral orgasm, but not the vaginal. Many feel that they are dysfunctional or that they're being shortchanged, but this couldn't be further from the truth. Men are even harder on themselves when it comes to the clitoral versus. the vaginal/G-Spot orgasm because they think they are somehow lacking in sexual prowess. Not so. A woman's body is unique, and no two are exactly alike.

The whole challenge with the G-Spot is finding it. Most men have found it accidentally, which is really the most common method of discovery. This chapter explains how to search (leave your Maglite out of this, thank you) and what it's supposed to feel like. Again, not every woman will be able to locate it, but half the fun is looking. If knowledge is power, then learning everything you can about the body female could only yield good things. But only use your powers for good!

Today's Topic: Body Image

As usual, it's your letters that inspire most of my topics, and this time I thought I would discuss body image. Why? Simply put, men have a much healthier attitude about their bodies than women. I have yet to meet a man that shies away from sex because his jeans were getting a little tight. "Gosh Doreen, I can't be with you tonight; my butt looks too big in this suit." I think you see where this is going, so let's try to slay the dragons of imperfection.

I don't mean to point directly at any one cultural phenomenon, but the fashion industry has not been kind to women. They present the public with a bevy of ultra-thin girls with no discernible hips to clutter the shot and expect real women to hold themselves against this idea of beauty. It's no wonder that eating disorders top the list of teen traumas, but it doesn't end there. Women are their own worst critics, and fall victim to something called "body dimorphic disorder." This psychological demon induces women to see a much heavier woman in the mirror (sort of like a fun house effect) which creates stress and of course, more eating disorders.

Most of the letters I receive on this topic explain how the sex became so infrequent that most of these couples just stopped trying. Most of these women know that their husbands love them, but they also fear that they're being pursued sexually out of duty instead of desire. I have no easy answers for this, but it does tend to cycle out of control. They gain weight, stop having sex, indulge in self-loathing, feel guilty about abstaining, gain more weight, and so on. Thus, the cycle continuously sprials. As much as I want to rally these women to just get back on the horse again, it's not that simple.

I'd like to share a composite letter that I've created from many different letters. It speaks to both men and women. Some were sent by the men about their wives, and some were from frustrated women. Both speak to this problem and how it can destroy sexual relations.

Dear Carmen,

My wife and I have been married for five years and just had our second beautiful child. My life is productive and fulfilled, but I don't know what to do about my wife. I still think she's beautiful, but ever since she gained 40 pounds with our last baby, she's been really depressed about her figure. I mean it would be great if she lost the weight, but not for my benefit-- for hers! It's like she equates who she is with the size eight I married, which couldn't be further from the truth. From the beginning we had mind-blowing sex, but since her weight gain, she's lost interest in having ANY kind of sex. When I ask her about it, she tells me that she's still attracted to me and can't imagine why I would still desire her sexually. Her answer for this was to just avoid sex entirely. Even in a dark bedroom she shrinks away from my advances. How do I convince her that she's still attractive to me?

I'd like to point out the real world. Look at the average couple. Most of us are not gracing the cover of *Shape* magazine, and yet dating continues. Physically imperfect people get asked out all of the time for several reasons. The most attractive qualities a person can posses are a positive attitude and confidence.

If you doubt me, simply look at some of the most beautiful women in the world today like Star Jones ("The View"), Camryn Manheim ("The Practice"), or Carnie Wilson. These women are all beautiful and exude confidence and sexuality, so just take a moment to evaluate yourself before you judge too harshly. Stay healthy and keep loving your partners no matter what!

♡ ♡ ♡ ♡ ♡ Reader Comments ♡ ♡ ♡ ♡ ♡

Dear Carmen,

Can I bring up weight issues? Not all men like toothpick girls. I for one love a girl with a few extra pounds. My wife isn't fat, but she's beautiful, and there is cushion for the pushin'.

[My buddy Mook from "Mook's Personals" has web addresses for *BBW*. You rock!]

Carmen,

I'm about two weeks behind on reading my e-mail, but I just felt I had to write to you concerning your column on body image. When my husband and I met over 15 years ago, I weighed 100 pounds and was between sizes three and five. We now have a 14-year-old daughter, and I stayed home with her the first five years until she started school. I started gaining weight almost immediately after I had her (even though I only weighed 110 after giving birth). I am now about 70 pounds overweight, which I know is not healthy, but I am working on losing the weight. I am doing this for me though, not for my husband.

My husband and I have a wonderful sex life. I asked him once how he saw me when he looked at me naked--did he see the "skinny" me or the "fat" me? He told me that all he sees is ME and he loves me, and that's all that matters. I count myself very lucky for having a man like this in my life. I know quite a few men who would have dumped their significant others if they gained as much weight as I have. I guess what we have really is true love.

Well, thanks for listening. I just wanted to let you know that I am one of the overweight women who still can feel sexy and enjoy a wonderful, healthy sex life. Thanks for your column. I really enjoy it and am even learning a few things :0)!

Dear Carmen,

Is it true that if you're not comfortable with your body you can't have an orgasm? I've heard that insecurities can get in the way of having an orgasm, and I know I have trouble having them. Is there something wrong, or is there something that I can do to help to have one?

[Relaxation is critical; if you're preoccupied with the finale you'll never enjoy the show.]

Carmen:

So what is the right thing to say when asked if her bottom's too big? (And it is!)

[Tell her it doesn't matter what you think; she's going to think it anyway. Then tell her if she's really unhappy, she should try a new workout routine, but (and this is a very important "but") tell her she's the berries no matter what! Good luck and go in peace.]

Dear Carmen,

I wonder if you would address a topic for me. My boyfriend and I enjoy a healthy sex life. We have been dating for eight months now. Our problem is this: neither one of us is the size of magazine models; we are both on the plus size. So unfortunately, we have a problem with his penis not being able to penetrate me far enough for me to reach orgasm. Could you suggest some positions that would allow for a deeper penetration, please?

[If a woman props her hips up on a few pillows, the angle is easier for the male to penetrate, and he doesn't get as tired holding himself in place. You might have to practice with one, two, or three pillows. You'll both know when you've hit the right formula. Best of luck, and I'd also like to hear from my readers about this, too!]

Dear Carmen,

After six years of marriage and over eight years of actually being together, my husband and I have added on the pounds. The best positions we have found for deep penetration are doggie, also with my husband on one foot and on one knee doggie. And woman superior but with my feet on the bed like I'm doing squats. This position takes a while to get used to because you will get leg cramps due to lack of exercise but is sure is fun trying! Thanks!

Dear Carmen,

For the reader who said she and her partner were overweight and found it difficult for him to penetrate deeply enough for her to reach an orgasm, try this: she lies on her back. He lies on his side on an angle so that his head is at 2 o'clock or 10 o'clock (depending on which side he wants to be), while hers is at 12 o'clock. He insinuates himself so that his penis enters her from behind her legs. Her legs can drape over his body. If his stomach is part of the issue, he can slide more into a 3 or 9 o'clock position. He can hold on to one of her legs as he penetrates, or she can simply leave them free. She can spread them for nice deep penetration or keep them a little tighter together if she prefers. He can still reach her nipples if he likes or stimulate her clitoris while she can pretty much lie back and ENJOY or pinch his nipples, since men enjoy this, too.

This position is comfy and not too strenuous for either partner. Both are in effect lying down, no one bears the other's full weight, and the penetration is very good. My partner and I use this position quite regularly because of the benefits. The only drawback is that you can't kiss while penetrating, but you can still have the closeness before and after, so it's not a problem for us.

♡ ♡ ♡ ♡ ♡ ♡ ♡ ♡ ♡ ♡ ♡ ♡ ♡ ♡ ♡ ♡ ♡ ♡ ♡ ♡

Today's Topic: Female Masturbation

Today I've decided to address an issue that has been whispered about, blushed over, and downright maligned for no reason other than discomfort. Female masturbation is one subject so replete with taboo that even close gal pals avoid talking about it, so it's time to roast a few sacred cows!

Before we can explore this area of female sexuality, I need to clarify that this issue relates directly to women and their ambivalence toward sex. Dating back to our Puritan training, we were taught that "good girls don't; bad girls do." Along with this archaic tradition came the idea that women should be taught and trained by their all-knowing husbands. With all due respect to husbands everywhere, this philosophy should have died with the use of chastity belts! Part of living in the 2000s means that girls from a young age should be taught a healthy appreciation for their bodies, which means exploration should be encouraged and not discouraged. If we can try to eliminate the guilt that accompanies masturbation, we would conquer more than just sexual inadequacy.

While it has always been more acceptable and even expected for young boys to masturbate, this too has had some drawbacks such as men who (out of habit) rush through sex for fear of "getting caught." Women who were raised with the "swept away" fantasy generally find disappointment when the event falls short of their fertile imaginations. If a woman has never been encouraged to explore her body and figure out what pleases her, what man could possible know what should work best? The idea is to familiarize young girls with their own anatomy by using proper names like vagina or clitoris instead of cute metaphors; my all-time favorite used by my great aunt was "goldie!" That still renders me speechless...

Sexperts feel that toddlers should not be stopped or shamed when they start to roam around their genitals; they too are intrigued with the sensation, so let them wander. When they get a little older, parents might suggest that they continue in the privacy of their room and to be direct and honest about what they're feeling. Girls who are reprimanded for masturbating are being taught that their genitals are naughty and should not be touched. If that's the pervasive attitude, how does this same young girl make the transition to a sexually confident woman? If you're one of those repressed women, allow me to make a few suggestions. Begin slowly with something common like the shower massage or scented oils, and work yourself up to something more aggressive...like a Harley. Now that's living large!

♡ ♡ ♡ ♡ ♡ Reader Comments ♡ ♡ ♡ ♡ ♡

Hi, Carmen, I just thought you would like this:

BEDTIME PRAYER FOR WOMEN

Now I lay me down to sleep, I pray for a man who's not a creep. One who's handsome, smart and strong. He's not afraid to admit when he's wrong. One who thinks before he speaks. When he promises to call, he doesn't wait six weeks. I pray that he is gainfully employed, won't lose his cool when he's annoyed. Pulls out my chair and opens my door, massages my back and begs to do more. Oh! Send me a man who will make love to my mind. Knows just what to say when I ask "How fat is my behind?" One who'll make love till my body's a twitchin.' He brings ME a sandwich too, when he goes to the kitchen! I pray that this man will love me to no end and would never compare me with my best girlfriend. Thank you in advance, and now I'll just wait, for I know You will send him before it's too late. Amen.

♡ ♡ ♡ ♡ ♡ ♡ ♡ ♡ ♡ ♡ ♡ ♡ ♡ ♡ ♡ ♡ ♡ ♡ ♡

Today's Topic: The G-Spot

I guess it was just a matter of seconds before I was going to be questioned about the infamous G-Spot. This is another one of those touchy issues that creates arguments everywhere. The reason for the controversy stems from the fact that its location is rather secluded and takes a little practice to find. Perhaps I can shed some light on the subject. Before I start giving directions like a town local: "OK, now y'all are gonna want to make a quick left by Crawdaddy's tree stump," let's clear the air. Nobody should engage in a night of amorous embraces with an agenda! You're not filing a flight plan, and the minute you make a mental blueprint, you should just call it quits. Remember that a healthy encounter begins in the mind. Gentlemen, if you're approaching the search for the G-Spot like Apollo 13, you'll only frustrate yourselves and your partner.

The G-Spot really does exist, but not all women are built the same so the location can vary by degrees. Invite your partner to explore your vaginal geography by suggesting various positions and stroking techniques. Ladies BE SPECIFIC about what feels good because you're not with a mind reader.

The best way to find it is by using your index and middle finger curled up like a small letter "J." Search the front wall of the vagina located closest to the pelvic bone and make small circles. She'll let you know if she feels uncomfortable...trust me. For some it's easiest to find if the woman is lying on her stomach. Remember it's different for everyone. While you crook your fingers up towards her navel you'll notice a rippled spot about the size of an almond. Some compare this tissue to a ripe strawberry texture as opposed to the smoother vaginal lining. For some, it feels slightly harder and becomes larger after stimulation. Male and female genital tissue is almost identical, so the response should feel like a small erection from inside.

If you're having trouble locating it, don't get frustrated. Vaginal tissue varies in thickness, and when it's stimulated, the engorged area becomes slightly more difficult to navigate. If your biggest problem is practicing over and over, you'll get no sympathy from me. Many women have never found their G-Spots so they're more likely to deny its existence, but it *can* be found if you're willing to experiment. Some women are more successful after they've located it themselves first and passed the information on. This requires a little more agility because if you're alone, you'll need to draw your knees up into your chest so you can find the right angle. If your fingers are too short, try something slightly longer that's easy to manipulate. If you're still having difficulties, try the "clock" method. Picture your vagina like a clock face and start at high noon. 90% of females tested found this position to be highly sensitive, while eleven, one, and four o'clock were also favored.

Naturally I'd love to know how your searches went. So if you are so inclined, send me an e-mail and let me know what worked for you. If it didn't work, then maybe I can gather some useful suggestions. In the meantime, happy hunting!

♡ ♡ ♡ ♡ ♡ Reader Comments ♡ ♡ ♡ ♡ ♡

Dear Carmen,

I wish I were a woman! Your instructions were great!

Carmen:

Correct me if I'm wrong, is the G-spot not the same thing as the clitoris? In which case, if it is, I have yet to have a problem finding it. It really does work. And oh my goodness, what results!

[No it's not the same thing at all, but I'm glad you're having fun!]

Today's Topic: Vaginal Orgasms

Today feels like a good day to cover vaginal orgasm, don't you think? Many of you have asked why it's so hard to have a vaginal orgasm, and some of my male readers are feeling slightly concerned that their women only climax through clitoral stimulation. While I'm not certain why this is considered a problem, relax, we can work through anything together.

It should go without saying that reaching the heights of ecstasy with your partner should be revered no matter how it happens, but some of you are stressing out over the almighty vaginal orgasm. Before you give this too much credence let me assuage your fears: it's all great.

The most common physical similarity among women involves orgasms; most women can only orgasm in conjunction WITH clitoral stimulation. "Training" the female body to experience all levels of orgasm involves patience, relaxation, and most of all, time. By nature, men were originally constructed to reach ejaculation quickly before they were eaten by a wild boar (or choose your favorite predator). Now that we've surpassed the hunter/gatherer stage, we can slow things down a bit. Most women have lived through the experience of making love to a really enthusiastic yet speedy man at some point. Yes, we can recover, but the anxiety left behind does not disappear so quickly.

The cycle begins with the man feeling inadequate because his partner didn't orgasm. In turn, the woman then feels guilty because she did not validate his sexual prowess. After this pattern has been established, each session becomes more goal oriented which only feeds the pressure to perform, and pretty soon the whole endeavor is doomed to fail.

If you can begin with an intelligent discussion about just letting it happen, you remove the stigma of performance anxiety. The next time you find yourself spontaneously making love, my suggestion would be for the man to penetrate her from behind (no, not anal intercourse), while fondling her clitoris with one hand. What she needs to feel is the freedom to orgasm however she can, while feeling you inside of her at the same time. In addition to having most of her erogenous spots covered, you are also creating a cradle behind her which covers her whole body, not just the vagina. It's important to remember that both men and women make love with their entire bodies, and sometimes the separation of body parts can make it feel rather clinical or pedestrian.

I'm not suggesting that this a panacea for vaginal orgasms. Some women are just not capable, which does not invalidate the experience. Many of you wrote about the difficulty you had finding your G-spot which is also common, but it doesn't mean there's anything wrong. I cannot stress that enough. Men are not measured by their ability to *give* a vaginal orgasm. By the way nobody is *giving* anything to anyone. Orgasms are shared and experienced, not given. As soon as you change the philosophy behind the act, the sooner you'll reach another level of intimacy. Let's remember that practice makes more practice? At least that's how I see it, right?

♡ ♡ ♡ ♡ ♡ Reader Comments ♡ ♡ ♡ ♡ ♡

Dear Carmen:

I've been a subscriber since August and have found your advice extremely helpful. My wife, who normally prefers to discuss sex in an indirect, if not demure, manner, has made several comments on how satisfying our lovemaking has been recently. I want to ask you a question on what is the most delicate of sexual subjects in my marriage. My wife seems unable to have an orgasm during intercourse, always preferring cunnilingus prior to this event. In the past, I have tried a few times to 'climb this Mt. Everest,' always to fail and leaving my wife feeling miserable and inadequate. We have discussed this, and she seems to feel that the majority of women have a very difficult time experiencing orgasm during intercourse. I am not going to set about proving this theory, if you get my drift. While this is not stressing our relationship, I would like to be able to achieve this most intimate of all sexual experiences. Can you provide some insight?

[She's quite right. It's perfectly normal for some women to experience only clitoral orgasms. There is nothing diminishing about this, and she shouldn't feel inadequate about anything. Putting pressure or expectations on the outcome will only make things worse. Relax and enjoy what you have together.]

Dear Carmen,

I am a 17-year-old female, and my boyfriend and I recently started having intercourse. I am worried that I can't orgasm without clitoral stimulation. It seems that's the only way I can have an orgasm. I noticed this when we started having oral sex. When he would finger me or perform oral sex on me, it would feel good, but I would never have an orgasm. He has only made me have an orgasm twice in the past five months, and I'm afraid there is something horribly wrong with me. Now that we're having intercourse, I'm wondering if I'll ever be able to have an orgasm. It worries me because I always make him have one. He's starting to feel bad because he can't do the same for me. Help me please, Carmen! I don't know what to do about this. How can I have an orgasm? How can I solve this? Is there some medical reason why I can't have one? I would appreciate a response from you as soon as possible because I have so many questions that need to be answered.

[It's very common to have climax difficulty; you need to relax and stop worrying. Perhaps your body and mind aren't quite ready for this yet. Just a thought. Stay safe.]

Today's Topic: Female PC Concerns

In the interest of saving my column from becoming too male "PC" oriented, I wanted to answer the other most-frequently-asked question from readers about the female PC. I'll begin by answering yes, there is such a creature, and there are exercises to strengthen this little love muscle. So, fear not loyal readers, it's time to cover the female concern!

Before we dive into this subject, let me just say that I was in no way giving special attention to the male PC. The reason there are so many steps to strengthening the male PC is because men must fight their primal message to spill their seed and concentrate on orgasm without ejaculation. Sounds easy, but it's no simple task.

Women also have a PC muscle which I can explain in a simple example. Gentlemen--have you ever had intercourse with a woman who was able to contract around your penis with her vagina by giving it a little squeeze? That's the female PC muscle in all of its glory, yet there are specific exercises women can perform to strengthen their muscles, too, just like men.

The pubococcygeus muscles in both sexes play an important role in sexual pleasure. For women they run from the pubic bone to the tailbone and encircle the vagina. Like any muscle group, the more you build responsiveness, the more you can enhance you sexual endeavors.

When men or women contract the PC muscle, it reduces the bloodflow in the surrounding area until you relax it. At this point there is a sudden increase of blood to the genital area which can prolong an erection for a male and produce greater lubrication in a female. Within this sensation lies an increased awareness of sexual arousal which can be, well, it's the whole point of the exercise, isn't it?

Enter trailblazing gynecologist from the 1940's Arnold Kegel. He was really the first to develop a series of female PC exercises (not surprisingly known as Kegels today). His original focus was for women with weak bladder control or incontinence so he thought if they could develop these muscles, it could ease their urinary distress. Like many great inventions, it also proved useful in other areas.

For women, Kegels begin by contracting and releasing the PC muscle, just like men. However, instead, think of bringing the walls of the vagina together in a slight kissing fashion, then release. You can vary the pressure and intensity, and before you know it, you will be doing this 100 times a day or more.

At this time I'd like to interject some really great ideas for how to kill time at the office. So, you're sitting in a conference room fighting sleep deprivation and boredom. Just think of the fun you'll have drawing the walls of your vagina together right under the nose of the CEO! It's not like anyone can tell, right? Imagine the odds of someone stopping a meeting to declare, "Ms. Jones? Are you listening to these new demographic changes, or are you doing your Kegels again?" Not likely, but thanks for indulging my fertile imagination.

At the risk of sounding repetitive, ladies, you'll have to build your endurance just like your male counterparts by holding these contractions longer and longer. You will also be asked to build more intensity as you progress. Whereas men might be visibly noticed wagging their PC muscles, women can do this in total privacy and solitude, so don't tell me you don't have time! This can be done in the shower, the carpool, the elevator, the principal's meeting, or in the dentist chair, so take your pick!

Now comes the more intrusive part. After you've established your Kegels prowess, it's time to improve on a good thing. Toys will be your next step to strengthening your PC muscle. A dildo or small weighted balls will do nicely. What you're trying to accomplish is "grabbing" an object within your vagina and hanging on with full force. It is important to remember the relaxing part as well. You will only achieve success if you hang on, followed by letting go. You shouldn't have to insert anything further than one or two inches before starting your exercises, but this is where I lose most women.

We all want to be more proficient lovers, but many women have real taboo issues with sex toys. Yes, they're willing to work on themselves isometrically, but the introduction of a foreign object (no, I don't mean Francois the waiter) causes stress. I can't help you overcome your reticence, but I can remind you that your body is your temple, and it's yours to improve and pamper as you see fit.

If you do not believe how easily accessible these toys are, just surf the web for two minutes, and you will strike oil! Please at least try the PC exercises. After all, you wanted your man to try, right? Turnabout is fair foreplay. Just try it for awhile, and you will undoubtedly notice the results. Give it a try and write to me soon.

♡ ♡ ♡ ♡ ♡ Reader Comments ♡ ♡ ♡ ♡ ♡

Carmen,

That muscle flex is also great for us ladies. It helps tighten the pelvic muscles in that area, helps to control that urgent dash to the ladies' room, and gives our mates the ultimate in pleasure also. We won't mention it also tightens your lower stomach to a great degree and makes you even look sexier, now will we? Hmmm?

[Sexier is always good!]

Today's Topic: Female Ejaculation

Once again I've stumbled into an area of misinformation concerning the female anatomy that was never discussed in your pedestrian sex education classes. I couldn't help listening to a heated conversation between two young men arguing about female ejaculation. The first guy swore on a stack of bibles that he had been with a woman who possessed this very talent, while the other one just dismissed his claim as bar bragging. So does this phenomenon exist or not?

Throughout history the concept and mystery surrounding female ejaculation has been approached as folk knowledge or myth. For years this area of study was suppressed and dismissed by the medical establishment. Dating back to the fifth century B.C., Hippocrates and his minions believed that conception could only take place if both the male and female fluids were mixed.

By the second century, Galen distinguished between the female "seed" and female prostatic fluid which contributed to sexual excitement. In keeping with these same findings, Dutch anatomist Regnier De Graaf studied this at length where he discovered that, "female prostatic fluid rushes out with impetus, frequently."

So what happened? Why did the concept of female ejaculation fall into disfavor? Probably because years later famous sexologists Kinsey and Masters and Johnson rejected the notion of female ejaculation by stating that women who claimed to have this experience were probably suffering from urinary incontinence.

When these same experts were then asked why this fluid was white and milky, the subject was dropped entirely. I wonder how they treated their challengers: "I don't care if it's white! Go to your room!"

As science advances, researchers have turned their attention toward this question. What they discovered was how similar the female and male genitals are. This is no surprise since all fetuses are identical until the sixth week in the womb. Both men and women have a PC muscle, both produce fluids when aroused, and both ejaculate. The reason for the confusion can be attributed to everything from ignorance to confusion.

Many women confuse their ejaculatory fluid as discharge or "spare" lubricant, while others just think it belongs to their mate. The biggest variable is how intense the experience is for each woman. Some report having explosive ejaculations and describe the wet spot left behind as more of a pool. Other women don't experience the same amount or intensity of discharge which means that for some, it's not as discernible. For all of my male readers, relax. It's perfectly normal.

Now that you know what is happening, aren't you just a little curious about how to make that happen? Much more on this subject will be forthcoming, but I would really like to hear from my readers. Do you have any female ejaculatory experiences you would like to share? Has this happened to you? Please send your comments and/or stories, and we'll talk ALL about it!

♡ ♡ ♡ ♡ ♡ Reader Comments ♡ ♡ ♡ ♡ ♡

Dear Carmen,
Thank you so much for talking about this subject. I appreciate that you discuss topics that others dismiss or ignore. My husband has been telling me for years that I ejaculate. I pretty much believed him, but in the back of my mind, I still was not sure and assumed it was urine. Thank you for addressing the confusion.

[Your comment echoed those of other women; it's supposed to happen, and it's not urine!]

Hi, Carmen,

I love your articles. They're quite interesting. I'm writing to say that I experience ejaculation. When my husband and I have a great session, I would be laying in a huge pile of my juices. At first I wasn't sure what was going on until I read an article on the subject. It's important for women to learn about it, so if it happens to them they won't be so self-conscious. Thanks for writing such great stuff. Keep up the good work.

Dear Carmen,

All women ejaculate, and all women are capable of orgasm. It is just ignorance and an uncaring partner that don't allow a woman to receive the full exhilaration of a sexual encounter.

[Can I get a hallelujah from the choir? You're right on the money!]

Dear Carmen,

Maybe with columns like yours more men will be educated enough to enjoy their partners' experiences so that only the selfish few will not assist their partner to achieve both ejaculation and orgasm.

[I'd like to think we're doing a real public service here.]

Dear Carmen,

In tantra, it's a widely-accepted concept that there is indeed female ejaculation and the fluid is called amrita, which means nectar, and it is distinguishable. I've never experienced it personally with my partners, but every time we make love there is a pool of fluid, and I know it isn't all me.

[I loved this e-mail because it proves that this audience is educated, articulate, and willing to share.]

Today's Topic: Female Viagra

I have to admit to being rather cynical about any product that claims to produce miracles whether it's about weight loss or baldness. So, it goes without saying that any ad that promotes a pill to fulfill your every romantic need ranks high on my suspicion list.

I can't even think about the term "female viagra" without images of some poor woman thinking she was misinformed about sex..."you mean I'M supposed to have the erection???!!!" We all knew it was only a matter of time before the whole viagra discovery was going to be distorted, twisted and misused. For the record, I think any drug that enables the male anatomy to succeed in its most ardent desires is GREAT! But, it's also been proven to work. It has saved relationships, started relationships, enhanced relationships and maybe even ended a few. The fact is, it works.

Enter the unscrupulous business folks who were groomed to capitalize on the success of one product by shamelessly promoting it in others. Suddenly the appearance of female enhancement herbs is flooding the market. I love the nebulous claims:

"For total female satisfaction"...

"Get the passion you've always wanted"...

"Improve your intimacy"...

"Red hot and ready for love"...

ENOUGH ALREADY! How gullible do they think we are? Obviously I'm referring to the products with no scientific data to support their claims. These are the ones that require money first, questions second. While I deeply believe that certain herbs or foods can create a more amorous disposition, I must draw the line at these claims that lead people to believe that all romance and sexual function comes in a bottle. I haven't heard from anyone who tried them; perhaps one of you could shed some light on this for us? Anyhow, when it comes to female sexual matters, it usually boils down to hormones or exhaustion.

I'm not trying to make a blanket statement. I realize that some women are just more aroused than others, but if any of my subscribers are asking me to endorse any of this stuff, the jury is out. My responsibility is to guide in the proper direction, so if you are questioning your sexual energy levels, scale, or interest, you must see your doctor first.

The reason these companies have a niche in the market is because most women who are too shy to consult their doctors would much rather make a discreet purchase over the internet than risk disclosure. They may be embarrassed and prefer privacy. This is silly because if your doctor can run a scientific test (check your hormone levels, etc.), then you are more likely to find a successful alternative.

If you're thinking about taking these herbs just for kicks, hey, it's your money so who am I to judge? Before I get off on a rant, remember that sexual dysfunction is generally a combination of things so try not to separate your body from your mind. Children, stress, depression, sleep deprivation, not to mention the condition of your relationship. All of these issues factor into how well your body is working or responding to passion, yes?

One last note to my male subscribers who keep asking me about penis enlargement herbs, drug, or systems: I think my answer is if these things really worked, we'd all be walking funny. Exercise caution before trying any product and for God's sake, speak to your physician first! Bless you all.

♡ ♡ ♡ ♡ ♡ Reader Comments ♡ ♡ ♡ ♡ ♡

Dear Carmen,

Ahh, but you repeat yourself. Children AND sleep deprivation are redundant.

[You are quite right. I stand corrected!]

Carmen,

I have some information you may want to share with some of the female subscribers. My father is a physician, and one night he and I attended a lecture about the use of viagra for women. The speaker was a female physician. Most patients that are on anti-depression medications often suffer from sexual dysfunction. This physician prescribes viagra for her female patients that have sexual problems. It has been reported from these women that viagra has invigorated their prowess. The problem is that most patients don't want to mention any sexual problems with their physician. I hope this helps someone.

[I'm sure it did; thanks for your input.]

Carmen~~

If you EVER find a doctor, male or female, who can truly help with one's sexual issues, please let us know under what rock they are hiding! I have NEVER found any physician to know beans about the nuances of sexual function, other than basic. On today's topic--female viagra--there is a vitamin supplement known to have very similar effects known as anatomy. If it weren't for reading non-medical books and e-mail lists, I wouldn't be finding any help at all! Keep up the good work.

[Calling all rocks...any takers out there?]

Carmen,

In response to this female viagra that's suppose to work so well, the only thing I have every found that works is good, honest communication and maybe a margarita or two. As I have always said, "The shortest distance between two people is communication." Use it well and the world is yours. Use it poorly and you are your only world.

[Well written!]

Carmen,

I'd like to hear your opinion on the insurance company's willingness to pay for viagra so that men can get an erection, while their reluctance to pay for birth control for women remains staunch. It's nearly 2001 and the needs of women still come in after the desires of men.

MY opinion is that it's big business, not our men in general. While I think women need to take responsibility for themselves, I *do* think our men do themselves a disservice in not being watchdogs on women's issues, too. After all, sex is a partnership issue.

[I'll try to be brief: HELL, YEAH! There should be equity for both sexes concerning funding.]

Dear Carmen,

My sister tried this. It doesn't work, but she said the yohimbe massage oils do wonders. I think it's more the massage than the specific oil, but if you have a medical problem which inhibits your sexual response, the female viagra is a joke. It's all about marketing, whereas the natural oils may help until medical science can understand and correct the problem.

♀ Chapter Six ♂

Open Up and Say "Ahh!"

I can say without hesitation that I get more mail about oral sex than any other subject. "How should I ask for it?" "Am I doing it right?" "How can I improve my techniques?" "Should I really do this?" It's amazing how much attention this subject gets (and if you live in a state where this is illegal, move on to the following chapter). You might be interested to know that many couples are troubled over approaching the subject with their partner. Apparently this has been the lynchpin between couples who haven't engaged in it yet, couples who want to, but are afraid of doing it wrong, or the infamous, "I want him/her to, but they won't even consider it!" Trust me when I say relationships have ended over this. Not because it's the end all and be all of sex, but if one partner refuses, the other may feel rejected or limited. Some feel that limitation goes further into the relationship than just the bedroom, so sometimes this can be a real can of worms.

We've included the articles about what feels good and what can feel too intense, so hopefully this will clear the air for those who are looking to try something new or for those who want to refine their skills. This is no different than any other aspect of sexuality because it's different with everybody. I'm just trying to discuss the options, not promote any particular caveat. This became such a hot topic that we ran a poll here to see who gives more and who receives more. Can you guess if it was men or women? Without giving up any surprises, I think you should give this chapter to the person in your life. Nudge. Wink.

Today's Topic: Oral Sex

Before I waste any time, let's consider the next few issues rated "E" for explicit. It would seem that my readers have made oral sex the most requested topic EVER! How to engage in it, how to improve it, how to approach it, and how to get your partner to at least try it has obsessed many of you. Hey, I'm not criticizing...far from it! Let's face it, this is a topic that deserves mass, in-depth coverage, so let the games begin.

What's so fascinating about deviating from the well-worn path of missionary sex? Besides EVERYTHING. Let's clarify a few basic facts. The mouth, tongue, and lips are capable of gymnastic feats that our genitals can only appreciate with awe and inspiration (and a few giggles). As intense as this experience can be, let's start with the most important aspect, which is attitude.

Most of the mail I receive revolves around couples who disagree about who gives and receives. This is pointing out the obvious, but it should go both ways. If you're not with someone who approaches oral sex like it was his/her last meal, you're going to have a problem. It's just like any other sexual activity; you either crave it or you don't. As for those who decided against it before actually trying it, keep an open mind. I say this because many of you have asked me how to approach the subject with their partner if he/she has not ventured south yet. It's not a matter of wanting one over the other; it's all about experiencing the full menu as opposed to always ordering the same thing. Don't be afraid to approach your partner with the idea. It's not about being unsatisfied; it's about exploring the other avenues.

In the interest of equality, let me just inform you all that according to the poll we conducted a few weeks ago, women give oral sex more often than men. That's right, women give it more than men. Why is this, you ask? Perhaps it speaks to the fear that most men have regarding scent and taste. Some men have had the unfortunate experience of dating women who were less hygiene-savvy, and it spoiled the urge to endeavor south EVER again. While I sympathize with the unpleasant memory, I have to throw some common sense into this discussion.

Have any of you ever been with someone who couldn't kiss well? Have you ever endured bad breath? Well, you didn't stop kissing other people, did you? A woman's genitals should taste as sweet as her mouth provided she showers on a regular basis and isn't harboring some unspeakable infection. Most women are aware of this so they keep clean and trimmed (which most men prefer).

As for the women who hesitate to give oral sex, the same rule applies to men. If your man practices good hygiene, he should taste good all over (and if he's considerate, he'll trim his pubic hair as well). If you're worried about gagging, remember that you're stimulating his penis with your mouth and not trying to swallow it whole. Additionally, women have to address the choice about swallowing or not swallowing his semen. Again, it's a personal choice. If you've never tasted your man, give it a try before you make up your mind. Some women are under the impression that he'll deposit a gallon of fluid, and you won't be able to take it. Relax, it's a quick shot and only about one tablespoon. At only six calories per ejaculation, you won't be violating your diet, either. If you've tried it a few times and think it's repulsive, then perhaps you should change your strategy, but try not to prejudge.

Now that we've talked about the taboos, the next few columns will address the actual strategies for the most satisfying fellatio and cunnilingus. In the future, you'll notice that I don't use the phrase "blow job" or "eating out." Neither is accurate, and it tends to sound crass or offensive. Until next time, keep an open mind and keep writing!

♡ ♡ ♡ ♡ ♡ Reader Comments ♡ ♡ ♡ ♡ ♡

Dear Carmen-

I have a very personal question for you. How do you politely ask a girl (a girfriend you have been dating for over a month or so and have been somewhat intimate with) if you can perform oral sex on her? And vice versa, how can you ask politely the same be done to you? HELP!

[Ease into the conversation while watching the movie *White Palace* starring Susan Sarandon and James Spader. There's a great scene about oral sex in this film which might make the conversation more natural.]

Dear Carmen,

Nancy Friday's book *The Secret Garden* gave the following statistics: 82% of the 26,000 women she interviewed had performed oral sex on their partners (for our own use, let's assume the partners were men); 67% of those women had oral sex performed on them. That leaves 15% who weren't reciprocated. Since I read that, I've been trying to even the odds. Hopefully, before I pass on to the great beyond, I'll get it down to perhaps 10% and will have to live a really long time to do that. But I'm trying. I like your column. Have you ever taken guest editorials? Thanks for listening.

[Consider you my first guest. I'd love to read your contributions!]

Dear Carmen,

I read an article that most men feel their partners stop oral sex too soon after they ejaculate. How long after ejaculation do you continue to stimulate your partner?

[That depends on your partner; some can continue right into your next session, but ask him first.]

Today's Topic: The Italian Method

Today's issue might just be the best of both worlds--blending safe sex with unbridled passion. Some of you have voiced your concern about the use of condoms and how it dampens the mood when you have to stop everything to unwrap your little latex friend. Fear not my amorous friends, I'm going to teach you about the Italian Method!

At the risk of sounding indelicate, the Italian Method is the application of a condom using your mouth. It has nothing to do with Italian men, nor did it originate in Italy. No, I don't know how it got its name.

Back in the day, "working girls" used this trick as part of their repertoire to keep themselves safe and their clients happy. It takes a little practice, but isn't that the whole point? Before you proceed, you need to be able to put your mouth in a flute position (like a baby kissing) and cover your teeth with your lip while you open your mouth.

1. Lubricate your lips with a water-based product.

2. Remove the condom from the package and hold the nipple between your thumb and forefinger so it looks like a tiny sombrero.

3. Put a jellybean-sized drop of lubricant in the nipple end of the condom. This assists the application over the most sensitive part of the penis and prevents that pesky stuck-to-the-top feeling.

4. Place the condom in your mouth gently with the nipple between your lips and the lubricated end towards him.

5. Hold the shaft of his penis in one hand while positioning your mouth at the tip. Allow the condom to rest at the end while you gently use your tongue to unroll it over the area.

6. While you unroll the condom down the shaft, it is important to keep your lips over your teeth to keep from tearing the latex. If you have braces, you're probably too young to do this anyway, so stop reading and go do your homework!

7. Go down the shaft as far as you can and finish with your free hand, making sure to keep the action smooth and without interruption.

It takes a little practice, so if you feel more comfortable trying this out on the zucchini or cucumber in your fridge, forge ahead. I'd like to mention that buying three condoms at a time would be appropriate because buying a gross might frighten the man you're with. If you know that intimacy is a certainty, cut the package open so when you're ready to rock, you won't ruin the mood with the untimely crinkle sounds the packaging makes. If you're really good, the man won't realize what you've done until its over. Now THAT'S a skill worth having! Send me your thoughts as usual, and we'll share some more wisdom.

 **Reader Comments**

Dear Carmen,

One thing you left out which is VERY IMPORTANT is the fact that this should NEVER be done with a condom containing spermicide. Spermicide will make the mouth, lips, and tongue go numb for quite a while. I don't recommend it.

Today's Topic: Cunnilingus

As promised I intend to cover many techniques for oral sex, both cunnilingus and fellatio. No, I'm not going to use slang because it will sound too cheap, so if you're ready for some straight talk about how to please a woman with you tongue, read on! As a side note, today's column works very well for my female same-sex couples, too. Enjoy. Some of you may want to avoid this subject entirely, but before you decide against it, let me say a few things. Your tongue and mouth are capable of doing more intricate maneuvers than the rest of your body. To be frank, women love oral stimulation, but not all can reach orgasm through cunnilingus. The giver needs to be reminded how sensitive the clitoris can be, so approach gently. The slower and softer approach will yield more results every time.

For women who prefer direct clitoral stimulation, you will have to lift up her clitoral hood which is akin to the male foreskin. Try using your index and middle fingers of both hands and run your fingers around the inside of her outer labia before gently lifting up and away from her clitoris. Some women will hold themselves open, so orchestrate according to your own needs. Lifting this prepuce will create a more taut, open space for your mouth to explore. (Are you still with me?) I don't mean to jump ahead; I'm just giving directions to those who already know what their women prefer.

Before we continue, let me just say that it's best to have some pillows under her hips and under your chest to allow for a better range of motion. As with most beginnings, her legs will probably be together. Keep her like this as an introduction to slowly opening her legs, which will increase her intensity as you move around. Don't forget that you can assist your mouth by eventually penetrating her vagina with your fingers simultaneously. This creates more pressure and pleasure, so remember to keep your fingers in slow motion and use small circular strokes. You'll notice her breathing becomes deeper and slower as you proceed. Remember to gauge her breathing and give her plenty of time to adjust.

For lack of a better model, think about how you lick an ice cream cone. You can use just the tip of your tongue before you take a big scoop on your tongue. For a more subtle approach, pretend you're eating pudding straight out of a container with no spoon. If you want to deviate for a moment, try to penetrate her vagina with your tongue. The extreme moaning should give you a clear idea that she's enjoying this. Her positions will vary slightly from wrapping one or both legs over your shoulders. To stay more connected, try approaching her from the top down so your chest is still touching hers (think about a pre-69 position), which enables you to relax your neck muscles by resting your head on her pelvic bone. The more patience you exercise, the more she will feel free to respond. Again, if you're not treating this like it's your last meal, she'll sense your reticence and shut down. I'll bring some more advanced ideas to the table next time. I'm suddenly craving ice cream!

Reader Comments

Carmen,

I was pleased to see that you are addressing the topic of oral sex with "taste" and humor. You stated that women perform oral sex more than men, so my man must be an exception to the rule. He's 46 years old; his health is not what it used to be. He's also a recovering alcoholic, so his libido isn't what it used to be, too. We don't enjoy intercourse as much as most people, but we augment our sex life with oral sex. He enjoys going south so much that he is the best I have ever had! I hope you will encourage men who have problems to try oral sex as a way to augment their own sex lives with their partner. We have always given and received on an equal basis; that way no one feels used.

Today's Topic: Beyond The Alphabet

Here's a stretch. I was at a backyard party with some of my favorite male friends who never fail to amuse me with their views on human sexuality. One was responding to the sex poll that confirmed the fact that more women give oral sex than men. As an aside, I'd like to say that every male at that party was baffled. Perhaps my friends are the anomaly, but all of them were enthusiastic about cunnilingus. To quote one of my more affable friends, "Hey! I weigh 250 pounds, there's not much I don't eat!" The question of the day was what can you do beyond spelling out the alphabet with your tongue?

Let me begin by thanking my friends for their honest contributions, their wonderfully open minds, and the fact that they'll share just about anything after a few beers. I love you all and wouldn't have as much fun researching without you.

So the question was what do we do beyond spelling out the alphabet during cunnilingus? The answer is slow torment. I'm serious! The technique that always yields great results is to slowly, slowly, slowly work your way to her "sweet spot." Just to refresh your memory, women take longer to arouse than men. One of the biggest mistakes men make when it comes to sex is rushing through foreplay. The way to avoid this is to redefine foreplay. Don't think about it as "pre" activity because foreplay *is* the activity. The longer and slower approach is always the best. Begin to think of foreplay as the best part.

If you're wondering how to measure where she's at in this process, listen to her breathing. It isn't the fast panting portrayed on soap operas that indicates total sexual arousal; it's deep, slow breathing. The key for women is always relaxation. The more relaxed she is, the more receptive she will be to more advances.

A woman may be wet and capable of penetration long before she reaches the deep-breathing stage, so don't just "check her oil" to see where she's at. Trust me, if she's wet at this point, she'll be saturated later. Just be patient. Due to evolution, men are genetically programmed to ejaculate quickly. The average caveman needed to "get

off" before he "got offed" by the nearest predator in order to perpetu-
ate the species. Thank goodness times have changed. Men no longer
need to expedite the process, so when it doubt, go slowly.

Before you just dive into cunnilingus, try caressing her back slowly
while she lays on her stomach. You can gradually move your hands
and fingertips to the inside of her thighs just stopping short of her
genital area. Continue to rub her GENTLY all over. The skin is the
largest organ on the body, so cover her entire body.

Women appreciate a total body experience, so if sex starts to feel
fragmented or isolated to just the genital area, the experience can be
greatly diminished.

While you listen to her breathing become deeper, brush your fingers
just slightly over her clitoris once while rubbing her back. The idea is
to visit her area periodically and not just camp out at one spot. The
same applies to your tongue. Once you begin exploring with your
tongue, make sure you trace her back, buttocks, thighs, back of her
knees, and the small of her back before you approach her genitals.

Once you've centered on her genitals, run the tip of your tongue
around the inside of her labial lips. Before you center your attention
to any one area, make sure you lock your fingers around hers so you
are connected in more than one way. Holding hands can also make
this a more intimate encounter that tells her that she's more than just
a naked body in the room to be played with.

Some women have incredibly sensitive genitals, and sometimes they
can't handle too much direct contact (nibbling or sucking) on the clitoral bud. Feel out if she's too sensitive before you proceed. If she's
willing, have her hold herself open to you so you can use your tongue

in an unobstructed manner. Deviating your attention to her whole body by taking breaks from the clitoris will also prolong her pleasure. I can't give you a perfect time frame to shoot for, but beginning with foreplay through orgasm, it could easily take one hour. If this sounds like an eternity, my guess is that you've been rushing for a few years.

She'll take more time with you in turn, and practicing this method will increase the opportunity for multiple male orgasms (always a goal). I can't encourage you enough to try this slower approach. Remember that the entire hour is not devoted to oral maneuvers (too tiring), but your hands and your touch will be doing most of the work. To borrow a phrase: if you don't have the time, don't do the crime. Best of luck!

♡ ♡ ♡ ♡ ♡ Reader Comments ♡ ♡ ♡ ♡ ♡

Dear Carmen,

Hey, I just had to reply to this one. I'm a guy, and I love going down on my girl. For whatever reason, it really helps me get turned on as well. Believe it or not, some of the best advice I ever got was from a Sam Kinnison comedy show. He said to lick the alphabet. And since I was in a motel room with a girl at the time, I had to give it a try. IT WORKS! Capitals, small letters, cursive, use your imagination!

Hi, Carmen,

You are 100% right. Gently and slowly is extremely important. So is teasing her with your tongue well before you get to the "prize." All women are different, but as a rule, if you listen to their breathing and observe moans and gyrating hips, you're doing something right. Remember where you get especially strong responses and revisit the area from time to time. I consider this at least as personal as intercourse.

Today's Topic: The Seal and The Ring

As the saying goes, turn about is fair play, so it's time to explore the many wonders of fellatio. To be blunt, I've NEVER met a man who didn't love this, but there's always a first time, I guess. Anyway, if you're interested in becoming more orally proficient with your man, let's get started.

I'm going to assume that you've made the decision to either try this for the first time or just fine tune some of your existing skills. I previously mentioned that some women struggle with the gagging potential or the swallowing issue. It's all a personal preference, and I am in no way promoting or endorsing fellatio or cunnilingus. I'm simply providing the information should you choose to indulge.

In order for this to be as comfortable as possible for the woman and pleasurable for the man, we need to cover some ideas that will relax the gag reflex. Take control of the situation by making the "okay" sign with your thumb and index finger and placing it around your mouth like you're going to blow through the hole. This will extend the length of your mouth by acting as the seal. The average mouth is approximately two to three inches in length, but the average penis is five to six inches long. No problem. Use the seal to apply pressure around the penis while it enters your mouth and release in small intervals. This will determine how far the penis enters your mouth, unless he suddenly pushes in too far. If this happens and you feel yourself start to gag, stop your mouth motions until the reflex passes, but keep your hand in motion so he can keep his erection.

At this point, you need to divert your attention so you can recover while keeping things in motion. Slow down and try to breathe deeply while you allow your palate to relax. Shift the angle of entry into your mouth by moving around; if you try to take his penis straight in, it will go directly to the back of your throat. (Do not pass "Go," move directly to gag!) Your best bet is to have your mouth approach his penis from above so you can be the one moving around on him. The soft palate is very flexible and can easily accommodate the end of his penis which naturally curves up and won't just automatically head south down your throat. He shouldn't have to try to move his hips around to where he wants to go; that's your job. Some of the reasons oral sex can be so stimulating for a man are so he can concentrate on the pleasure point without exhausting his leg muscles, arm muscles, or worry about any of the other aerobic activities. It's all about his needs, and with a little practice, you should be able to choreograph your own special dance that keeps you both happy. The seal acts like an extension that gives him the deep throat sensation without having his entire penis in your mouth.

Yes, there are many other techniques for oral sex that I intend to cover in the future, but like any good teacher, I like to start with the basics before I move into the more advanced courses. Before I end today, I'd like to remind you that this technique feels great when your man is fully erect, but try it when he's still flaccid and work him into "full attention" as an appetizer. Trust me, he'll love it!

 **Reader Comments**

Dear Carmen,

The reader who commented that enjoying yourself while performing oral sex on your partner is critical is 100% right! It's not a chore, it's part of making love, giving yourself and your partner pleasure and excitement. Learning to relax and feel good about giving oral is the best gift you can give. Of course, that goes hand in hand with cleanliness and making your sex inviting to the other. My girlfriend goes wild when she smells a little drop of cologne she told me she likes down there!

Dear Carmen,

I thought this sounded absolutely yummy! I just wanted to share:

Chocolate Cherries Jubilee

It's amazing how much pleasure you can derive from a single chocolate-covered cherry. Here's a fantastic technique guaranteed to satisfy his sweet tooth--and all the rest of them, too.

Here's what you need:

One chocolate-covered cherry. Here's how you do it: get your man naked. Have him lie on his back. Turn the chocolate-covered cherry upside-down and bite off what is now the flat portion. You should now have a chocolate "wafer" in your mouth and be holding a chocolate cup filled with juice and a cherry. Bite the wafer into halves and set one half on each of his nipples. Hold the cup above your man's legs and tilt it so that the juice drizzles down along both of his inner thighs. Do not let the cherry fall out. Using your mouth and tongue, slowly lick the juice off your man's thighs. He will find this incredibly arousing. Now place the cherry into your mouth. Give your man a deep, long, passionate kiss. Push the cherry into his mouth. By now, the chocolate on his nipples should be melting. Using your mouth and tongue, suck and lick it away from each nipple. Finally, turn the chocolate cup over and place it on the head of his penis. Then pleasure him orally. He'll discover that life is a bowl of cherries!

Dear Carmen,

I just wanted to say thank you to the person who suggested the chocolate-covered cherries and eating them off each other. I tried this on my boyfriend, and he went crazy. I think we're going to buy stock in Brach's candies because we love the new use we've found for them.

♡ ♡ ♡ ♡ ♡ ♡ ♡ ♡ ♡ ♡ ♡ ♡ ♡ ♡ ♡ ♡ ♡ ♡ ♡

Today's Topic: Oral Sex Etiquette

I know this may come as a shock to you all, but I was having a conversation with one of my dear friends about sex. How unusual, right? Well, as with all of my reader mail, some of the most provocative questions come from friends and subscribers. This time I thought I would ask some questions about oral sex etiquette.

Sometimes people just crack me up. What I mean is they often behave in ways that fly in the face of reason. For instance, if two people are intimate enough to share something as personal as oral sex, why do some shy away from kissing while making love? I've received many a puzzled letter from readers who tell me that their partner won't French kiss after or during oral sex. It doesn't stop there, either. Some complain that after they have traditional intercourse, their partners won't taste them afterwards. Why? This baffles me as well, but I can tell you that these kinds of sexual stipulations can ruin a relationship. I think we've established that intimacy does not just happen from the waist down, and if you've been practicing oral sex thus far, I can assume that hygiene is firmly practiced, right? Well, if there's no problem with that, I can only assume that your partner is afraid to taste him/herself, which is a shame.

It is time for me to preach about accepting your body sexually, which includes reminding you that once you've learned rule number one, know thyself, you should eagerly anticipate sharing your glorious self with someone wonderful. Part of learning about your sexuality includes getting familiar with your own body chemistry. Most of you know you sweat, so you probably wear deodorant. Sex is just like that, only you should know your own scent. Some have a sweet, musky smell, and some lean towards the salty side. No matter what you are, you should be comfortable with your attributes and be willing to share.

One of the concerns I wanted to address was the mixed message of "I want to have sex with you, but I don't want to taste it after we've mixed together." To Hell with that sentiment! If you love someone, you're supposed to love all of them. Refusing to kiss or taste someone during or after only leaves one of the partners feeling ashamed of him/herself, which is not a healthy message. One letter in particular summed up the focus of the problem: "when he refuses to kiss me after we've had oral sex, it makes me feel cheap and whorish like he would only do that with someone he was married to." The problem comes down to trust and love. If you don't want to have a shared experience, stick to masturbation. If you want to reap the benefits of a highly-charged intimate coupling, then take it for all it's worth and stop putting limits on your endeavors!

♡ ♡ ♡ ♡ ♡ Reader Comments ♡ ♡ ♡ ♡ ♡

Dear Carmen,

Wow! I wish I had a job wherein I received requests for oral sex. (Sorry, my wife is an English teacher.) Come to think of it, she gets lots of requests for oral sex, too. Cheers

[I guess I should have specified that the requests were for advice and not the actual endeavor but...]

Hello, Carmen,

I was reading about oral sex in your column and had a question. When talking about trimming pubic hair, are you suggesting cutting it some or shaving completely? I am in my 40s and am still learning a lot from your column. Thanks.

[It really depends on the person. Some like to trim; some like to shave. I guess it's a matter of trying each option to see what you or your partner prefers.]

Dear Carmen,

Why do guys like the shaved pubic hair thing?

[There's a simple explanation: you can see her genitals more clearly, and the sensation of skin with no hair is also a turn-on.]

Carmen

As a man of advancing years and modest sexual experience, I've been amazed at the number of otherwise intelligent, knowledgeable and meticulously-hygenic women who have no concept of proper feminine hygiene. It is obvious that they bathe regularly, but it seems they bathe "across" their genital area. I suspect they simply have never been told, nor otherwise considered, what abundant odor-causing bacteria can be harbored between the folds of their personal rose petals. Worse, they may have been taught by their Mommies "not to touch" there.

When I have encountered such a situation, I've simply added a shower or bath (together of course) to the early agenda and given her the pleasure of having it done sensually for her. Usually, this is all that's required and can be accomplished tastefully (pun intended) and without offense, while letting her know of both the need and the solution.

Of course, the same occurs with, and applies to, men, especially those of us who are uncircumcised. I DO love my daily shower, especially being single and unattached. Often, it's the only sex I get.

♀ Chapter Seven ♂

Thank You, Come Again

It's not just for women! While it's always treated with a little skepticism, almost everyone is fascinated with the idea that men can also experience multiple orgasms. This chapter is really for every couple who has experienced premature ejaculation or the two minutes of ecstasy when it could be two hours. Don't take on the exercises with a vengeance, either. It's not about vindication as much as it's about education. I'm always amazed at how many men know so little about their bodies and what makes them work. If you don't know your own parts, how are you supposed to service them? Once you discover which muscles to develop and how to do it, you'll never look at lovemaking the same way again. I have quite a few readers who write in concerned about their lack of staying power, and they're always relieved that there is something they can do besides think about baseball until they can't hold off any further. I have a friend who thinks about his mother-in-law's mustache just to stave off ejaculation for a little while. The trouble is that sometimes it does too good a job, and then he doesn't finish!

Before reading about how to perfect this, you might be surprised to find out that orgasm and ejaculation are two separate events. Most people think this is one event because one follows the other so closely. If you're at all curious about this, read on and make up your own mind before you dismiss this. This also goes back to the ancient Taoists, so if you want to argue with ancient wisdom...

Today's Topic: Multiple Male Orgasms

Today is the first edition of "Great Sexpectations" where I'll address the facts, fiction, and fantasy of our too-often maligned primal nature. From serious romance to casual titillation, we'll cover it all, and with your feedback, it is my mission to blow the lid off of sexual repression and expand your horizons. Enjoy!

That's right, I said males. Now, before you injure yourself speeding to the keyboard to inform me how impossible this is, read on. Sex researchers are finding that orgasm has more to do with the brain than it does the body. Beginning with the ancient Taoists who were the first to make the distinction between orgasm and ejaculation, these practitioners of sexual Kung Fu were interested in sexuality as a means of men's total health. They wanted to study the exhaustive and depleting physical effects brought on by physical ejaculation.

Because most men experience orgasm and ejaculation within seconds of one another, they often confuse them as one in the same. They are not. Preadolescent boys are able to achieve five or more orgasms within a short period of time, even while sleeping when there is no physical stimulation taking place. This information led Kinsey (of the famous Kinsey Report) to argue that "climax is clearly possible without ejaculation."

The working definition of a male orgasm is roughly the same as it is for women: "rhythmic body movements, increased heart rate, muscle tension, and then a sudden release of tension, including pelvic contractions." The idea of nonejaculatory orgasm is probably foreign to most males, but don't be too dismissive. I know what you're thinking: "Carmen, we're already responsible for initiating sex (I'll get to that soon enough), orchestrating the choreography, and holding back long enough to bring our women to orgasm. Now what?"

Fear not. I'll be discussing the various techniques that have taught men how to separate the two acts so they can learn the benefits of achieving multiple orgasms and improve their already fabulous skills!

I encourage letters, feedback, tips, questions, stories, or anything else you'd like to share with me. Just send an email and thanks for sharing!

Reader Comments

Dear Carmen,

I just would like to say when I first saw this, I started shaking in my chair, not because I don't believe it, but because my husband does it a lot. We will have sex, and he will get off, and then without any down time for me, he starts again and goes until he gets off again. There have been times when he has done three times in row. We were both worn out after that, of course. I am surely not complaining. I think it is cool that he can do that, but the second and third time around do not last as long as the first. They seem to be a lot more intense. I think it may have something to do with the fact that after the first time, he is so sensitive down there, and it just drives him wild. So I know it can be done, and believe me, it's a wonderful thing.

[Some men are just natural at multiple orgasms; the rest have to practice a little, but it's certainly worth it.]

Dear Carmen,

Thanks for the tips, but I gotta tell you my fiancé already mastered this technique. Let me tell you he's 63, almost 64 (I'm 39 going on 40), so you men out there, don't give up. It can be done, and to the women out there that would be the lucky recipients of this lesson, all I can say is WOW. I have never been so satisfied in all my life.

Today's Topic: Training Techniques for Multiple Orgasmic Males

The last issue of "Great Sexpectations" was the first time we dove right into the controversy surrounding multiple male orgasms. Not only are they possible, but there are definitive exercises men can practice to further their stamina and satisfaction. If you think having a more intense sex life is worth a little effort, read on!

When the ancient Taoists questioned the debilitating aspects of "post-ejaculatory stupor," they were looking to maximize their health by preserving their energy, i.e. sperm. The answer was to practice non-ejaculatory sex. Once a man learns to separate orgasm from ejaculation, control becomes key.

The PC, or pubococcygeus, muscle located near the prostate is the same muscle used to start or stop urination. The stronger this muscle becomes, the more control a man has over his release time. The first exercise entails the practice of stopping urination midstream. This may sting or tingle a little at first until you get used to it, but after a while this task (while sounding unpleasant) becomes easy to perform. I was also told by a close male friend that suspending a towel from an erect penis is a great way to do pull-ups by "wagging" the towel up and down. That's not half as funny as *where* he decided to loudly announce his terrycloth prowess: in a semi-crowded bar where the audience seemed amused, yet appreciative of the info!

The next step entails training the intense buildup of genital energy to circulate through the entire body away from its obvious destination. I can just hear the doubt as I write, but allow me to reiterate; sex starts in the brain! Your best bet is to find a suitable partner with whom you have a deep level of trust and passion, or it is not as likely to work. A drunken encounter with a stranger is a poor first endeavor. You must learn to channel this energy by deep breathing, or belly breathing, which swallows the urge to ejaculate and disperses the stimulation throughout the body. Just exercising these two techniques (and there are many more I intend to cover) will yield a marked improvement in your stamina and, of course, your confidence.

It is my most profound desire to improve romantic endeavors everywhere, but research does not take place in a vacuum, so I need to hear from my audience about any and all issues you wish to address in this column. While you can get a lot from talking with close friends, I feel there is a certain advantage writing about your concerns where your anonymity is protected. Take a risk and write to me at the e-mail address below, and together we can bring sexual closure to the masses!

♡ ♡ ♡ ♡ ♡ Reader Comments ♡ ♡ ♡ ♡ ♡

Dear Carmen,

I have enjoyed your newsletter and read it enthusiastically! I am a 46-year-old female, and my partner is a 28-year-old male. We have been seeing each other for over a year and have yet to tire of each other both sexually and socially. I had been married for many years and never had the chance to explore my own sexuality to it fullest. I have a wonderful man. He has such a healthy sexual outlook, and he has helped me blossom into my true self. He is multi-orgasmic, and the sex we have together is spectacular. I feel beautiful and very happy with my body and sexuality. I am a very lucky woman. I want to reaffirm to your readers that yes, men are multi-orgasmic, and I have found a gem.

Signed, NO NAME because you will all want him. HA HA HA !

[I for one always wind up dating younger men so there must be something about this, huh?]

Today's Topic: More About the PC Workout

I need to provide an explanation about how this column is produced. Most of the time I'm about a week or two ahead of my readers, so sometimes it's difficult to carry a theme in order. I have recently outlined our new project to explain the complete PC workout for men, wishing to extend their performance time. Today we will cover some of the exercises in the regiment. Take a deep breath and begin!

Before we describe the exercises, I'd like to address the women who feel threatened or intimidated by this program. Some of my female readers are under the impression that men seeking to become multiple orgasmic will become machine-like and insatiable. This is not true. Exercising the PC will simply increase a man's knowledge about his performance while strengthening his endurance. These exercises are meant to bring you closer together and enhance your intimacy.

The first exercise needs to be practiced three times a day. Flex your PC muscle 20 times for one or two seconds at a time before releasing. That's it. Squeeze it 20 times a day, EVERY day for three weeks. You'll notice this becoming less tiring almost immediately.

The next phase of these exercises is designed to be your little secret because it can be done anywhere without detection. It's essentially the same as the first (squeezing/releasing) while sitting at your desk or on the bus. You might be able to hold your contractions slightly longer than two seconds by now, so go ahead and increase the time, but don't over stress the muscle.

Your squeezing prowess should be strong enough to move into the real death-grip phase. In addition to the 20 short squeezes a day, add 10 SLOW contractions as hard as you can at five-second intervals. These are very intense and might be difficult to maintain, but they will get easier. As intensive as it sounds, this should only take two to three minutes a day. It's a minuscule amount of time for some really great results. Don't forget that anything that's good for the PC is also good for the prostate. It's also important to stick to your schedule like any other work out.

I need to warn you about the two most frequent mistakes concerning the exercises. Doing too many reps can stress or strain your muscles, so go slowly. Some falter under the "no pain, no gain" philosophy, which doesn't apply to this area. The second error is failing to isolate the PC. If you're doing it right, your stomach, upper thighs, and buttocks are all completely relaxed. If they're tense, you haven't isolated the PC, and you will not reap any rewards for your trouble or dedication.

Now that you have the plan to improve your PC strength, next time we can discuss how to implement these changes in the bedroom. We'll talk about practicing with your partner and what to expect during this transition. Don't worry; it's all good. Until then, squeeze your way to a better love life!

♡ ♡ ♡ ♡ ♡ Reader Comments ♡ ♡ ♡ ♡ ♡

Carmen,

I will agree that multiple male orgasm is not only attainable, but easy, too. I am a male reader of yours and am 19. No, I couldn't always have mmos, but I learned quickly with the Kama Sutra or a version thereof. There are some positions that can keep a man on edge for minutes instead of seconds. So, I was able to gain control on my own with towel-ups. Print this so that all the males know that you're not just spouting gas at 'em.

♡ ♡ ♡ ♡ ♡ ♡ ♡ ♡ ♡ ♡ ♡ ♡ ♡ ♡ ♡ ♡ ♡ ♡ ♡

Today's Topic: After Priming the PC

Today we're progressing beyond the PC exercises to the first plateau of multiple male orgasm. In a previous edition I explained exactly what this means, but the topic always brings new readers and fresh confusion. As a courtesy to my new readers, I'd like to briefly outline what this entails.

Whenever I discuss the practice of multiple male orgasm, it's greeted with a barrage of questions, doubts, curiosity and humor. There are more misconceptions about this than there are about the female G-Spot. To be precise, multi-orgasmic men can have two or more orgasms in a row without resting, i.e. without the flaccid, resting phase. By resting I mean the post-orgasmic time when the penis is not easily aroused. A multi-orgasmic man can maintain an erection between sessions and can continue three, four, or more times without resting. It's usually at this point in the conversation where people start rolling their eyes and scoffing at the idea. As a matter of record, there are some men who naturally possess this ability without any practice. Some of these lucky few are young, but many keep this ability well into middle age.

How is this possible? Many doubt this because the standard experience shows us that most men experience what's called "post-ejaculatory stupor" (an expression that is hard to forget). It is during this stupor that most men are prone to pass out. This can also be a sensitive point for women if they haven't achieved orgasm yet. I need to stress that this is not meant as a rejection, nor is it lazy behavior. Women often fail to understand how totally depleting ejaculation is for men and misunderstand the exhaustion for lack of consideration. Not so.

So how is multiple orgasm possible? This is where the PC training comes in. After you've prepped the PC, you're now ready to learn how to have an orgasm WITHOUT ejaculating. Orgasm and ejaculation are not the same physical act. By exercising the PC muscle, men can achieve orgasm without riding the wave all of the way through to the ejaculation. It sounds tricky, but with a little practice it will become second nature. Most men pair them together, so this concept can be met with slight trepidation.

It's at this point that you need to connect with your significant others to plan on a few changes. This will yield some terrific results, but both of you must agree to try this together. If the idea appeals more to one than the other, the exercise becomes a moot point. If you bring your minds together, your hearts and bodies are sure to follow. Learning to become multi-orgasmic starts in the same place as any healthy sexual relationship, which means three things: attitude, commitment, attitude. Next time we'll discuss the techniques for separating orgasm and ejaculation. I promise this will all make sense.

♡ ♡ ♡ ♡ ♡ Reader Comments ♡ ♡ ♡ ♡ ♡

Dear Carmen,

I don't think I will ever be able to thank you enough! I subscribe to your Great-Sex e-mail, and if anything comes along that I think would interest my boyfriend (I refuse to say partner; it's so impersonal), I forward it on to him. Well, I sent him your PC exercises a little while ago and thought nothing more of it, until last night. He had been doing these exercises, and we had the best sex of our relationship! He had much more stamina than usual. My orgasm was much more intense, as he had more time to focus on me, and his orgasm lasted for minutes, rather than seconds. It's made such a change. Thank you!

[Thank you for sharing.]

Today's Topic: Arousal Scale

One of the problems I encounter with this column is trying to capture a physical sensation with words only. Remember when you were little and you found out if you were a visual learner versus an auditory learner? Well, this subject entails the third type of learner, the tactile method. You know, as in hands on? I'm going to try to help you qualify some of the questions you've posed.

I've officially lost count of how many e-mails I've received asking about levels of orgasms or arousal. Let's begin by describing an orgasm like a sneeze. Could you describe every nuance of a sneeze in detail and have it make sense in print? Perhaps, but something would be lost in the translation. One of the most frequently asked questions I get from both men and women concerns orgasms. Most of you want to know if they're different or if they differ in terms of intensity. The answer is yes to all of the above.

Have you ever had to sneeze really bad, but you're perched at the brink of almost? When you finally get it out, sometimes it's a small yet shallow victory, and other times you almost blow the roof off of your house? Yes, clever reader; you see where this is going, but I'm having so much fun with the metaphor.

Arousal and orgasm are very similar to this in terms of intensity. Some of you want to know if orgasm feels the same for both men and women, and from what I've read, the answer is yes. No, I've never had a penis, but doctors agree that the sensation is very close because genital tissues are almost identical for both sexes.

Before I try to give you the scale, let me just add that even if they're markedly different, neither side is complaining, right?

Okay, now transport yourself to the grocery store on a crowded Saturday, and you're doing battle in the produce section. Right now your arousal level is at one, which means zilch. Not only are you not feeling any excitement, you're trying not to be outwardly hostile to the winging old woman who keeps getting in your way (some of them are so good at that).

Keeping our story in the grocery store, you see a hot looking guy who just parked his Harley. Let's name him Steely. Steely will be my male demonstration model for the remainder of the scale discussion. Steely just found something he liked in the bread aisle and starts to tingle. He's at level two or three which is that point where a man feels a change at the base of his penis, and he's starting to wake up.

Before you know it, Steely's at level four (near the ethnic foods). He's worked himself towards that low level arousal that's definitely starting to feel good, but he could stop without too much trouble. Deciding that he might not want to stop at level four, he charges ahead to level five or six (by now he should really be making tracks to get out of the check-out line before his agenda becomes too obvious). At this stage he's really into it and has no intention of stopping.

Level seven or eight means that Steely should be somewhere private and hopefully soundproof. His heart is starting to pound and his face is flushed from the excitement. Talking also proves difficult at this point because you're rather winded or out of breath. Yes, this would be total hard-on with a plan.

Level nine has phases to it. You're reaching the top of the mountain, and you've found your pacing rhythm, and it feels exhilarating. Level nine starts out like this until the outside world just starts to disappear. You're losing your grasp on reality and nothing short of nuclear warfare is going to stop you. I'm not going to sidetrack into the PC exercises to slow this down because we're just trying to get through the levels.

Taa-daa! You're now at about 9.5, the point of no return. It's when you are certain beyond a shadow of a doubt that you are going to have an orgasm. The big "O" is on the way, and it feels inevitable. Nine point nine is where you have a psychological change, and nothing is going to make you surrender this feeling. This is the point where multiple orgasmic men have learned to maintain. This is why it's worth the effort. Nine point nine feels awesome, so we're learning to prolong this for both men and women. For the record most women can easily prolong 9.9, which is why we like to keep going and going and going.

Well, the only number left is 10, and that's obviously the climax in our little story. So what happened to Steely? I can't really give you any details, but I'm sure he's riding with the wind in his hair and a big smile on his face. Who knew it was double coupon day at the store? So, I hope this number system gives you a handle on your levels of arousal. To my one reader who is just obsessed over orgasmic intensity: I hope this helped. I've gotta go; my nose is starting to tingle!

♡ ♡ ♡ ♡ ♡ Reader Comments ♡ ♡ ♡ ♡ ♡

Carmen,

Females have varied intensity of orgasms, from the Big O to "waves" and multiples. Do men have different intensities of their orgasms? Or is the ejaculation intensity the same each time? Thanks, Curious

[Yes. Men experience many levels of intensity as well. Remember that all genitals start out the same in the womb for the first six weeks, so our feelings are surprisingly similar.]

♡ ♡ ♡ ♡ ♡ ♡ ♡ ♡ ♡ ♡ ♡ ♡ ♡ ♡ ♡ ♡ ♡ ♡

Today's Topic: Learning How to Peak

I hope you enjoyed learning the arousal scale (at least you'll never look at the grocery store the same way again, right?). Well, as usual, there's a reason for learning those levels because you'll need to use your new wisdom for control purposes. Once a man learns his body signals and limits, he can make progress toward becoming multi-orgasmic.

I'll have to draw from yet another helpful metaphor in terms of arousal levels. If you recall from last time, I compared orgasms to sneezes. I swear it made perfect sense in the right context. Anyhow, the whole point behind learning your levels is so you're able to discern when you're going from one to the next. If you know beyond a shadow of a doubt that you're leaving level five and secure at level six, the next step is to reverse the process. Why?

Simple--once you learn how to peak, you can indefinitely prolong your erection. To practice, you need to let your arousal rise to a certain level, then let it fall back down. Think about blowing up a balloon and letting the air seep out a little at a time. Once you drop down two or three levels, you build your arousal again, only each time you try to peak at higher levels. Let's say you peak at six and let it fall to three. During the next wave your objective is to peak at seven and so on.

The real challenge is to perfect the level nine peak. To refresh your memory, level nine is the brink of orgasm prior to ejaculation. Once you have the ability to peak at nine, you not only strengthen your PC muscle, you can now learn how to plateau--maintain a certain arousal level. Remember that peaking involves letting the levels drop.

In order to make this exercise more efficient, you need to communicate your discoveries with your partner. Let him or her know when you're at level four or five or six. If you both learn this together, the practice should yield faster results. Some may find learning how to peak an exercise in frustration at first, but it's very normal to feel confused for the first few sessions. Once you get the hang of how to peak, you can build on this awareness to master the plateau exercises.

I guess I should explain that plateaus enable men to maintain an erection efficiently. I have to qualify the word maintain because it's not like keeping an airplane in a circle pattern over the airport until the pilot has clearance to land. When men learn to maintain their erections, they also maintain the arousal and the excitement that accompanies it. One of my friends started to equate this endurance with getting calluses on his feet so he could run longer. Wrong! We aren't working towards desensitizing the experience; we're working toward a heightened awareness to enhance sex. Next issue, I'll furnish you with the exercises to maintain a plateau, but for now you have something else to practice, don't you?!

♡ ♡ ♡ ♡ ♡ **Reader Comments** ♡ ♡ ♡ ♡ ♡

Carmen,

Now this is something that truly interests me. It seems that sometimes I cum and shrink, while at other times I either don't cum, or cum and can continue performing, which means I have it half-way down pat. Could it depend on the height of sexuality? Whether the woman is making me hot or not? Or just whether I'm tired or full of strength or a combination of the two?

Curious and Ready

[Sex is like a snowflake; no two endeavors are exactly alike. If you can remember something extraordinary that made you lose your mind once, try it again.]

Todays Topic: Perfecting Plateaus

Before we continue to scale new heights with peaking or plateaus, I need to address my female readers. It probably looks like I've totally dismissed your needs, but that's the furthest from the truth. Because the practice for becoming a multiply orgasmic man is for BOTH parties involved, I have to stress how important it is that you tackle these endeavors together. Practicing should be a pleasure and not a chore, so with that in mind, let's get started.

I recently discussed certain techniques for peaking by hitting one level, reducing your arousal, and building it back up again. Some men find it easy to achieve by taking deep relaxing breaths, but others can simply change their focus and decrease their progress. The whole point of the peaking exercise is to move toward the plateau stage. Building your skills always comes in a series of small steps. You need to assemble all of the ingredients before baking the pie.

Plateaus are meant to prolong arousal rather than decrease it, but up until now, you've slowed yourself down by taking small breaks, changing your breathing, or changing your focus. The plateau exercise should always be a demand-free task. In other words, both partners should engage in this for mutual pleasure and not results. It's the pressure we put on ourselves to achieve results or to perform that adds undue stress to sex.

After several issues where we have engaged in hands-on practices, it's time to experiment with actual intercourse...FINALLY! Before you get the idea to jump into this exercise, consider the most successful position for plateaus. The woman should be totally comfortable and lying on her back. Prop one or two pillows under her hips to achieve the desired angle. The reason for this is so she can bend her knees while spreading her legs and not stress her lower back. It also elevates her pelvis so access is less stressful for the man. The man should be on his knees between her legs keeping his arms free. This enables him to use his hips as his center of gravity which keeps his arm muscles free. One of the difficulties men have with using their arms is that intercourse becomes a series of erotic push-ups, which can tire out most men prematurely.

Once you secure your collective positions, remember to progress through the stages of arousal without any expectation. You should enter her vagina after you reach a stage seven or eight arousal, but remember that there is no such thing as too slow. Without exerting anything but your pelvis, slowly move your penis inside in small increments. Focus on the sections you're moving from the rim to the shaft, and let your partner experience her own levels of arousal as well. Learning about your bodies together is the most satisfying way to get closer in your relationship. Continue this together just like you would if you were peaking, only this time you have to stop the action with your newly-strengthened PC muscle. There are three good ways to utilize your PC, but the best way to remember it is to think of it as ABS car brakes. When you reach a stage and want to maintain it, you can try:

1. One long, hard squeeze or...
2. Two medium squeezes or...
3. Several quick short squeezes.

You might need to use a combination until you figure out what works best, but be patient. You'll understand your best method quickly. It's important to remember not to plateau more than four times at first because you can stress your penis and find that you can't ejaculate this time around. Don't panic, it's just your body getting used to prolonging the activity. You're not causing irreversible damage, either.

Once you learn to plateau at various levels, you'll want to incorporate other methods with the PC squeezes. The most effective combination for you might be to squeeze while changing the position of your penis inside of her. Perhaps you're thrusting quickly with your entire penis. Try a squeeze while slowing down and using only the tip of your penis, etc. I have to mention the level nine plateau. Because you're almost at the point of no escape, you'll have to really squeeze your PC. At this level, your best bet is one very long and hard squeeze, rather than the series of short ones. It sounds complicated, but I promise it will all make sense after a few sessions. Write to me and let me know how you're progressing or if you're having difficulty. The upside to all of this practice is if you have trouble with the plateaus, you'll just have to suffer through a few pesky orgasms while you try! Not a problem. Best of luck!

 Reader Comments

Carmen,

I learned to separate orgasm and ejaculation about 20 years ago when I was a young marine. It is a wonderful companion to sexual positions that stimulate a woman's G-spot. The combination of these two techniques is very powerful. It has allowed more than one woman I know to "discover" she is multi-orgasmic. It is very satisfying to be able to take a woman to a new level of pleasure. As a bonus, their close friends also look at you with a God-like reverence.

Signed,
Short, ugly and popular

[Semper Fi!]

♀ Chapter Eight ♂
Proceed with Caution

One man's disposable is another man's treasure, or something along those lines. Anyway, we put this together on behalf of all of the water coolers, private restaurant tables, locker rooms, and pajama parties everywhere. For some it's only discussed in theory while for others it's a work in progress. Just as an observation, I find those individuals with robust sexual appetites to be less shocked by these proclivities and rather accepting of everything. You would do well to not pass judgment on those who do, rather than those who don't. To each his own, and I think what two people seek behind closed doors (or video camera) is really their own business. I've tried to approach all subjects because part of this forum means including everyone, including their diverse tastes. The whole idea was to get it out of the locker room and onto the Internet where it belongs!

On a more serious note, I've heard from readers that there was nobody else discussing how sensitive these new curiosities can be, and for many any departure from the standard is really more of an emotional risk, so it should be treated with deference and respect. Yes, this includes the subscriber who wrote to me about how sexy he felt wearing elbow length satin gloves. Who am I to judge? I did of course ask if he would be wearing them after 5:00 p.m. These aren't topics you would discuss in your "Rockwellian" moments, but they do exist, they are out there, and not everyone thinks they're bad! I think we should embrace the slightly left of center by bringing it out into daylight. Bring your sunglasses.

Today's Topic: Anal Sex

As usual, I have decided to respond to the largest audience request for this week concerning the question of anal stimulation and/or sex. Many women have expressed their concerns about how "normal" this practice is, and many men have questioned if this desire is related to subconscious homosexual tendencies. It's time to bring this subject into the light and remove more taboos.

First of all, we can't have an intelligent conversation about anal sex without addressing who your partner is. Any activity two people wish to share to satisfy their desires is perfectly legitimate! Try to avoid passing judgment on something if you don't know what it's about first.

Anal sex has been around since the dawn of time. Some began this practice when the female menstrual cycle made vaginal sex more difficult, and some just stumbled into it because the room was poorly lit. Whatever the reason, you must know that the anus is one of the most highly sensitive areas in our bodies, and the amount of nerve endings present can make for a highly erotic experience.

If you decide to venture into any kind of anal play, it is important to consider the length of your fingernails. Run your fingers over your nails to make sure there are no sharp edges and trim them according to how you yourself would like them to feel. The anus is incredibly tight at the entry point, so rough fingernails could make your "ooooh" moment into an "ouch" one instead. There is no natural lubricant in this area, so it will be necessary to lubricate your finger first with either your own saliva or a water-based lubricant.

Use gentle pressure and start slowly by massaging the anus in small circles. Next, try penetrating the area with one finger at first and use a gentle one-inch curving motion. The curve should follow from the front to the back of the body and not side to side. For men, this most closely resembles the G-spot in terms of sensitivity. The proximity of the finger to the PC muscle and the prostate heightens the sexual sensations. This takes place during oral sex or even standard intercourse if you really want to drive him toward stimulus overload. Massaging this male G-spot might be new to you, so relax before you try it. This kind of intimacy is best between two caring partners with no sexual reservations. If you feel it's too taboo to try, you're probably not going to enjoy it very much. Nervous tension can ruin most encounters. On the other hand, you might feel and hear a response like you've never heard before which can be the best turn-on of all. As usual, I'd love to hear from my readers about this, so keep writing.

 ## Reader Comments

Dear Carmen,

This is a touchy subject for most people. My longtime boyfriend and I have recently been experimenting with anal sex. At first I was disgusted, but I changed my tune shortly after. My question is this: we alternate between regular sex and anal sex. Is it safe to switch back and forth? Thanks a million for the great tips and strategies.

[No, you shouldn't go from orifice to the other; it's not sanitary. If you feel a change coming on, change condoms before going from vaginal to anal or vice versa. GREAT question. Thank you for writing!]

Dear Carmen,

I think you need to tell the woman who asked about anal sex (just in case they are not using condoms as contraception), that the man should actually wash his penis before switching gears/orifices. You also may stress the fact that she can get infections. (only because "not sanitary" may not be enough for some people)

Today's Topic: Bi-Curious Behavior

As usual my readers have created a new category of questions about being bi-curious. In this issue, you'll see a letter from a female reader that provided a real learning opportunity for this column. She not only addressed a common problem, but she asked some very normal, intelligent questions. After I write about this in detail, I invite my worthy readers to offer their thoughts, and we'll cover this issue in a special edition of reader comments.

To begin with, I'm not here to judge or preach about anything. I'm here to discuss valid concerns about human sexuality the best way I know how and offer a forum where we can muddle through ANY issue. If you are in any way homophobic, I suggest you stop reading and tune in to the next issue.

This letter detailed something so common that it was almost easy to skip over, but I didn't because she was speaking for many people who have written to me about this same issue. She started by confirming that her bisexual curiosity was now fully realized, and that she wanted to try to visit a gay night club for the first time. In addition to nervous anticipation, she was going to have to travel to a large city because she had not yet gone public with her feelings. Small towns can be brutal when it comes to anonymity or any real privacy, so this was her first problem.What made her letter so worthy was how normal and honest her fears were. She wondered how she should act when she got there, what she should do, expect, or fear. What I found so alarming was how similar her concerns were to everyone else's, straight or gay.

Do any of you know what to expect when you go to a singles bar? Of course not! You all have the same fears. What should I wear? How do I approach somebody? What do I do if I'm approached? Is everyone going to be staring at me? Will I look obvious? What if nobody talks to me? Am I making a mistake? All valid questions, right? Well, I'm not an expert on alternative bars, so I asked some friends. The only thing I was told more than once is that some gay bars can entertain slightly more aggressive patrons when it comes to pairing up. Her list was comprehensive, but I thought we should talk about being yourself. This sounds really "Leave it to Beaver" simple, but how do I dispense such pedestrian advise to somebody who is just beginning to sort out his or her identity?

The answer was an oversimplification for something that could be more complex than a standard heterosexual scene. After reviewing her options, I decided she couldn't go wrong if she showed up exactly as she expected to feel--nervous and insecure. Have any of you experienced being uncomfortable somewhere with only your obvious self-conscious body language wrapped firmly around you? Yes, but somehow God sees fit to put other people on this earth to help us through.

My honest feeling is that someone at that bar will know all too well how scared and insecure she feels and might just offer a kind word, some company, or a shoulder to lean on. Just because it might be another gay woman doesn't mean anything except that she should follow her inner voice the way she would with anyone. Feel her out to see if she's just offering a friendly gesture, or if you make a deeper connection, follow your instincts. This might not fill you with confidence, but you don't lose your ability to read people based on gender.

The other part of this equation surrounds physically going to a public place. If this woman is not ready to come out in Smalltown USA, how will she feel about being seen by a friend-of-a-friend? This is nothing to just blaze over; it has serious consequences. If she is not ready to deal with the fallout that accompanies small town gossip, she might have to put this trip on hold. I'm addressing my audience who has true bisexual or homosexual feelings. If you're one of those individuals who thinks dabbling in the bi-curious makes you sophisticated or worldly, save your efforts. Your endeavors to prove yourself open-minded or exciting to the opposite sex will just prove annoying to those who have real needs. Experimenting for the wrong reasons can end up in emotional distress for both parties.

I'm not sure if this makes these decisions any easier, so I'm sending out an "all call" to my loyal readers to ask for help. If any of you have a personal story to share or some advice, write in, and I'll print a special edition of reader comments covering the bi-curious concerns, fears, and answers. Remember, we're doing this together. That's the whole point of this column.

Reader Comments

Hello, Carmen!

I loved your article! My question is do you seduce a woman like you seduce a man? I'm bi-curious and want to have sex with a woman so badly. The problem is I'm not "out" in the small town that I live in, so I don't really have access to other gay women. The closest city to me is Memphis, TN, and it has plenty of gay clubs. So when I get there, what do I do? Please help before I burst!

[I don't think there are any hard and fast rules. Just be yourself and when you get to these clubs, do what you normally do. Make eye contact, conversation, and be open to what happens.]

Carmen:

I have been dating this great guy for three months now. I recently met a few of his friends, and I am sexually attracted to one of them. It just so happens this person is female. I've never had an experience with the same sex, but I have thought about it. Of course my boyfriend loves the idea. I have to admit that I am extremely curious and would not mind being with her, but I do not want to ruin things with my boyfriend. I know I could not handle seeing him with another girl and wonder if he would be able to just watch and keep his hands on me only. Is this a risk I should take and possibly ruin a good thing? I definitely want to spend the rest of my life with a man and not a woman, but I would not mind trying something new. Would I be making a mistake if I propositioned this girl?

Curious in Illinois

[My place in the universe is not to judge (nobody should), but if I had to make any suggestion, it would be for you to follow your inner voice. If you're feel this is an experience you were meant to have, then proceed. If your hesitant or afraid, follow your instincts. Gary Zukov would have a more eloquent answer, but above all, remember that you have instincts for a reason.]

Today's Topic: Fetish or Interest?

Here's the most common phrase written in my subscriber e-mails: "Is it normal to...?" This preoccupation with normal behavior and sex seems to be crucial to self-esteem. When a subscriber asks me that phrase, he or she is really asking me if they're alone, or if there are others like him or her out there. In almost every case I can assure you all that we share certain proclivities and shouldn't feel awkward about them. To the man with the wife who sneezes when she's aroused: I have no clue about it, but I'm sure that somewhere on the planet there's another man with a sneezing spouse...

Along with asking about what "normal" behavior is, I get several questions about why some things turn other people on. Now, this column doesn't cater to the fetish or porno crowd, but I thought I could offer a definition to qualify when something is of interest or if it's a genuine fetish.

First of all, we throw that phrase around without thinking. "She has a shoe fetish" or "he has a fetish for long hair" would be part of normal conversation. For the most part it's used as hyperbole and not as an accurate statement. Some are finding the dividing line a little blurry.

From the dictionary: Fetish - An object believed to have magical powers, especially of protection or - An object of unreasonably excessive attention or reverence or - Something as a material object or an often non-sexual part of the body that arouses or gratifies sexual desire.

I think only the last two apply to human sexuality. Most of you write to me when you get to stage two. You usually find yourself drawn into some pattern that happens on an unconscious level, but it's getting harder to ignore. For example, someone recently wrote to me that they were really turned on by men with long hair. This fact alone doesn't make it a fetish, but more of a preference. If this same interest becomes the primary focus for sexual attention and it must be present in order for gratification to take place, then it's becoming more of a fetish.

The pattern usually establishes itself in little steps. At first you might have remembered a titillating night involving hot candle wax. It was exotic to you at first, but you didn't have to have it in order for sex to take place. After the candle wax insinuates itself into your regular routine, you might want to question it. This is not to say that everyone with a fetish entertains it every time, either. Most of us enjoy ice cream, but we don't have to have it at every meal.

I think the largest concern about fetishes revolves around finding other people who have this same fascination. Trust me--they exist and you're not alone. Yes, there are fetish web sites that cater to every, and I mean EVERY, proclivity out there. If it would calm your fears, you might want to check it out. I'm almost certain that "foot" tops the list of most common fetish, but when Lewis (editor of "Bizarre News" www.bizarrenews.com) covered this, he actually found people who were aroused by crushing bugs! What can I say? Mine is not to judge...

I think if you listen to your inner voice for longer than a microsecond, you'll know in your heart if you're entertaining a real fetish or if you just have an interest in certain body parts. Remember, it's not just body parts, but parts that aren't usually associated with sexual arousal like feet or elbows. I can see it now: I'll get 50 letters about how sexy elbows are. Before you write, let me clarify that yes, the whole body is exciting, but a preoccupation with places that aren't usually erogenous are the ones we're talking about here.

On the other side of the coin, try to relax before you write to me about how much you love your partner's butt. That's not a fetish, it's a part of the body associated with sex. If I had a dime for every man that found female breasts sexy...you know the rest. Try to define your own guidelines and remember that you're not alone. I have to fold some laundry now. Don't read into it! Everyone loves the feel and smell of warm laundry... right?

♡ ♡ ♡ ♡ ♡ Reader Comments ♡ ♡ ♡ ♡ ♡

Dear Carmen,

This is in response to the man with the wife who sneezes when aroused. When I was 16, I had two friends (both were female) who claimed to sneeze every time they thought about sex! So no, he's definitely not alone. By the way, I love your column! Thanks for all the great advice, and keep up the good work!

Dear Carmen:

I, too, have the strange behavior of sneezing when I am aroused. It began almost 30 years ago during my free love "acid" phase one night when my girlfriend and I were tripping together and decided to make love. Suddenly the sensations I experienced were so overwhelming even my sinuses were stimulated, and I sneezed several times. This apparently rewired my brain somehow so that ever since I sneeze when aroused. Personally, I like it.

Carmen,

Re: sneezing while aroused. I have learned that if during intercourse the woman sneezes, you get a very strange sensation. This also occurs with hiccups and coughing. After a year in my relationship with my fiancée, I had a terrible case of allergies and a cold. We could not stop laughing hysterically. We had never felt that before, but it was great! Sex is not always serious, assuming both people are comfortable with each other. Just have fun. I study psychology in an amateur fashion (I study textbooks I pick up at yard sales and starving students), and my understanding is that the definition for fetish is when such becomes your primary sexual motivation, or oddly, your only one.

As such, it is possible to have a breast fetish. Some guys can only be turned on by that part of the anatomy. Similarly, there are some who can only have sex from behind the lady.

The odd thing is that fetishes are largely a male thing and are terribly arbitrary. For some reason, guys seem to be wired to imprint upon the first objects associated with sexuality, such that an early experience can easily decide the rest of your life. In contrast, women are very rarely fetishists and are more likely to be stuck on the whole role-playing bit. But you could have known as much from reading any lady's advice column, I guess. Anyhow, just my two cents.

Dear Carmen,

Would it be considered a fetish if you want your man to wear over-the-elbow evening gloves during sex? I also like big, bangle bracelets, and corsets.

[Forget the fetish definition. What do you think about female impersonators? I'm not being flip; cross-gender people are very titillating.]

Carmen,

I am e-mailing you in regards to certain fetishes. I will admit that I have two. Okay, I admit it. One time I was at my boyfriend's house, and we were watching a porn. The women on there were telling their boyfriends to spank them. I was like, "How lame." I was thinking, "What could be so great about that?" The next time we were messing around, he just did it, and oh my gosh, it was AWESOME. I'm not sure why, but it just felt good. My other fetish is a food fetish. Whenever we're messing around, I jack him off with my feet with whip cream, pudding, or honey, and then lick it off. I never knew I had fetishes like that. Finally we just started trying different things. I would suggest to anyone to be open. You never know--what might seem stupid, might end up as your fetish!

[Point well taken!]

Dear Carmen,

Your column is ALWAYS interesting, if not bizarre. I am not a lesbian, bi, or a fetishist, but am really turned on by my boyfriend who is a frequent and most convincing cross-dresser. We frequently go out together to women's clubs where he is hit on, then come home to make out as two girls. Except for shoes, we are the same size 9. Am I crazy?

[Not crazy; you just have a healthy appreciation for changing places.]

Dear Carmen,

I have a fetish with eyelashes, ears and noses. People think that's weird, but that's what turns me on. Also, is it bad for me to not want my boyfriend to masturbate? It's my biggest pet peeve ever, but it's important to me that he doesn't.

[Preferences have no rules; you are who you are, period.]

Hi, Carmen,

I really love your newsletter. I have to share with you what my fetish is. It's HARD HAT'S! They drive me absolutely crazy! It's such a symbol of "man." And whenever I see one on a guy, I get so aroused. Kinda funny in a way, but they can even distract me on the road! I just wanted to share this one with you, Carmen. Keep up the great newsletter. Happy Holidays to you...

[Don't get me started on construction workers. They make me purrr!]

In response to the woman who found hard hats arousing: I find yarmulkes arousing. To my knowledge, this is a pretty unique interest, but for some reason, whenever I see a Jewish guy (or any guy, really!) wearing a yarmulke, I get all excited! I hope this is normal because I cannot think of any rational explanation for this interest.

Carmen,

You sound a little stressed out. I have been reading your column for some time now, and I really enjoy it. I agree with everything you said in this last one, but I detect stress. I wish you a Merry Christmas and a Happy New Year. Ask your female readers how many of them are okay with cross dressing. It could start a new subject. You never know. Anyway, I love your column.

[STRESSED??? ME?? Oh, God, is it that obvious?]

♡ ♡ ♡ ♡ ♡ ♡ ♡ ♡ ♡ ♡ ♡ ♡ ♡ ♡ ♡ ♡ ♡ ♡ ♡ ♡

Today's Topic: Toys in the Attic

Well, it finally happened. I, Carmen, sworn to avoid all Tupperware, Candle, and Pampered Chef parties had to host her own. However, my party featured intimate products that you can't find at the grocery store. I know it must be a stretch to think of little me hosting a sex toy party, but it was all in the interest of research, right? Are any of you buying this yet?

It all started out as an innocent gesture to help a friend who just started working for this company that specializes in erotic products. Harmless. To my surprise, most of the products were quite reputable, and the presentation was very impressive. The advantage behind this little marketing gem was based on common sense. Most people are too shy to wander into their local "naughty store" to purchase anything controversial. Shyness seems to be a running theme with my readers, so in the interest of promoting a more open attitude about sexuality, I'd like to describe the evening and give a thumbs up to some of my hands-on research.

My representative (we'll call her "Lady J") had all of her products lined up and ready to sample, with the express directive that no men be in attendance. It's not a sexist issue; it just means that women are more receptive to these products if they're surrounded by other women. Some of my guests also happened to be teachers who had no desire to run out in public and purchase furry handcuffs under the auspices of students or PTA members. Get it?

Anyway, the evening began with the usual array of appetizers, chitchat, introductions, and of course, WINE! None of us actually knew what to expect, so we were ready for anything. Lady J reminded us not to be too scathing or critical if we saw something extreme because someone in the room might be purchasing it later in the privacy of my den behind closed doors.

The products were displayed in order from least extreme to battery operated. Some of her novelties had utilitarian appeal like body lotions and bubble baths, but it got interesting as soon as she pulled out the "nipple creme." I questioned the necessity behind a special creme just for nipples until I realized that it was designed to keep them erect. Let me just say that most women who have endured a winter in Chicago could see the humor in selling an Eskimo a refrigerator, but we were curious so we applied it with reckless abandon. It worked!

Next we moved into the sheet sprays, shower gloves, and erotic pasta shapes. Pretty soon the mood went from skeptical to genuine enthusiasm. On the surface, the sex toys seemed contrived or obtuse, but after you've been surrounded by them, you start to develop a healthy appreciation for the more creative aspect of a vigorous sexual appetite.

Once again, I'm not insisting that anyone run out to purchase a vibrator, but if you keep an open mind and get over the humorous overtones, you might just develop an interest in these items. At the end of the evening, she pulled out the Cadillac of all vibrators and placed it in the lid of the box. She turned it on low speed, and we all watched in wide-eyed amazement as the apparatus started its happy dance.

When she turned it up, I questioned the efficacy of something that could mix paint or beat egg whites, but I refused to pass judgment. After the laughing subsided, my friends disappeared behind closed doors to purchase their treats in private. Normally the customers would exit the room with their plain brown bags neatly stapled shut, but not my friends! Most of them ran into the living room to unveil their goodies like children dumping their Halloween bootie on the floor. We passed our toys around and promised to give a review when the opportunity availed itself.

So, my final word on this endeavor is thumbs up! It's a great introduction to the world of sensual products, and if you've never had the courage to explore in public, this is the perfect opportunity. Write back and share your favorite "toy stories" with me. It'll be fun!

Reader Comments

Carmen,

I have to admit I am not very knowledgable in the world of sex toys. My husband and I were just married about six months ago. I was wondering if you would go into more details for me about what's out there. You did mention some things in your article, but I was at a loss for what they were for. It would be greatly appreciated.

[I think I mentioned many products, but if memory serves me correctly, I talked about nipple creme which is used to keep your nipples erect. The other products were various vibrators that are hidden inside of a latex penis. Most people use these for vaginal penetration while simultaneously having oral sex. Some women who are not currently in a relationship use them for masturbation.]

Dear Carmen,

I've been reading your articles since they started. Some are very informative, and others I know about. Even if I've "been there, done that," I always seem to learn something. You're doing a great job at this, KEEP IT UP! Granted, I am single and alone, but I always want to learn new things and find new ideas for when that special whoever comes in my path, LOOK OUT! Anyway, I really wanted to tell you that the "Toys in the Attic" article hit home the most. Back in July, I had gone to my first toy party. I HAD A BLAST! Almost everyone who attended works with me, and we STILL talk about what we bought and if we like it. The picture you painted about your party is EXACTLY how mine was. What a hoot. Okay, I'm done. KEEP UP THE GOOD STUFF; I'LL BE READY!

[The phrase "some assembly required" shouldn't scare anyone anymore!]

Dear Carmen,

I have a strange question and story. Have you ever gotten a story or heard of men who use a vibrator to climax? My husband bought us a vibrator to use with me, but we were experimenting the other night, and I just laid it on his penis. He started getting really excited, and before I knew it, he climaxed with just the vibration. I couldn't believe it.

[Surprise surprise!]

Today's Topic: Subconscious Fantasies

"The conscious mind allows itself to be trained like a parrot, but the unconscious does not, which is why St. Augustine thanked God for not making him responsible for his dreams." - Carl Jung

There is something universally intriguing about fantasies. We all have them, and most of us don't understand them. It's very important to make the distinction that there are different types of fantasies. Some exist to vent something in a healthy nondestructive way, and some exist simply as wish fulfillment. No, I am not a trained psychoanalyst, nor am I a psychologist, but I have received many letters asking for my two cents about why we fantasize. Some people question why they fantasize even though they're perfectly content in their relationships, while others express frustration over their partner's fantasies.

Fantasies are strange creatures, so you can't find fault with your partner for having them. It doesn't always mean their needs are going unfulfilled or they're harboring secret feelings for other people. It doesn't ALWAYS mean anything. Fantasies can be a separate entity, or they can be incorporated into the conscious mind.

For example, you might dream that you were naked and riding a zebra bareback through your office. Somehow I doubt this is a reality that most of us want to experience (that would be a column for a different day), but I might be able to talk about some of the more common types. If you're lucky enough to hook up with someone who would gladly make the steamy ones happen, more power to ya!

Some defy logical description, while others skirt the boundaries of good taste. If you are one who harbors something too extreme, you might not want to share it with your partner, not because you should keep secrets, but if there's a chance that it might damage your relationship, you might want to curb it. I get hundreds of letters from readers who are asked by their partners to try something that they are not comfortable with, but they consider doing it for the sake of pleasing their lover. If you know you're involved with someone who would do something beyond their boundaries just to please you, please respect your better judgment.

It appears that women are expressing themselves more completely and without apology. Some are from a generation when it was impolite for a lady to discuss her sexuality, let alone her wants. Because sex is more openly discussed, the floodgates of repression have been unlocked, and things have really changed. It is the woman who suffered repression who can sometimes lean toward the angry or sadistic fantasy. Those who were silent are now the first ones running to the dance floor when they hear "Closer" by Nine Inch Nails. For those of you who don't know this industrial classic, the chorus (screamed in total angst by Trent Reznor) repeats the phrase "I want to F*** you like an animal." Pretty stern stuff and yet both men and women will lip synch this with reckless abandon. What does this say about levels of aggression and sex? Probably that everyone has entertained not saying the phrase, but acting on it. It's not supposed to be harmful, just passionate.

Many women (and not just the angry ones) have expressed fantasies where they exercise total control over a group of male slaves. They range from rough sex while the man is tied up, to starving them until they beg for salvation in the form of food, water, or sex. I'm not creating these; I've read them, and some are just brutal. The details are not as important as the reasons why. You can't control the subconscious; it somehow works to alleviate or vent things in a less destructive manner. No, of course not all women are angry. Some just have soap-opera-like fantasies about being totally seduced or being the seducer.

Male fantasies have traditionally been granted an audience through pornography. Yes, most of this industry is geared toward men and not because they're pigs. It's always been more acceptable for men to explore or discuss their fantasies, and unlike women, they can admit to being visually stimulated. They don't have the same amount of anxiety over renting something staged. However, women are still more comfortable reading or writing about it.

Neither gender is wrong. Each side has subconscious desires, but they don't exist because something is missing from the relationship. Some should be shared and others should stay quietly tucked away in your mind. I would, of course, love to read about yours, not the actu al details, but if you have them or if you allow yourself to think about them. It's an equal opportunity activity, 50/50 men and women, but I'm not sure what I'll get. I could go on, but I'm restricted by a sense of good taste, and I'm starting to freeze. I need to ride my zebra out of here and find a blanket. My colleagues are starting to stare.

♡ ♡ ♡ ♡ ♡ Reader Comments ♡ ♡ ♡ ♡ ♡

Hi, Carmen, it's me again.

I think it is wonderful that you are including playful, but seriously folks, tips in your newsletter. My husband and I have a few "games" that FREAK-OUT my friends when we share them, but THANK us for after they try. Here are a couple of our favorites, if you care to share them with your readers:

We play strip poker. No touching or sexual contact of any kind is allowed until the last piece comes off. (Sometimes I lose on purpose, just to see him squirm.) :-)

Write every body part down on a piece of paper, tear them out individually and throw them into a hat. One partner draws out a piece of paper and devotes an entire minute to the attention of that one body part (doing whatever--kissing, licking, massaging, etc. of their choice). Put the paper back in the hat, and it's the other partner's turn. We actually set a small timer. Take turns going back and forth until you just can't stand it anymore.

Skip the morning shower routine and opt for a shower together. This has actually turned into a morning ritual in our house; it's the perfect way to start the day connected.

[Thanks for the ideas; you guys rock!]

♡ ♡ ♡ ♡ ♡ ♡ ♡ ♡ ♡ ♡ ♡ ♡ ♡ ♡ ♡ ♡ ♡ ♡ ♡

Today's Topic: Office Romances

Sideways glances over the water cooler, discreet visits to the bathrooms, or the "accidental" brush while passing through a doorway. It's the white elephant in the room that everybody sees, but nobody is talking about. It's high time we talk about office romances. Warning: this subject may be treated with levity or perhaps humor. Please adjust your expectations now.

It's always complicated and never an easy situation, yet it happens all of the time. To set the stage we work longer hours and have less time (and energy) to socialize. Suddenly our whole world revolves around just one sandbox where we work, live, socialize, and sometimes sleep!

I am by no means saying that all office romances exists out of convenience (although some are guilty of this). It's more complicated than that. Just by the amount of time you're exposed to your coworkers, you find yourself noticing things on more of a personal level. Little nuances that you shouldn't really be noticing, like the curve of an eyelash or how broad his shoulders are when he handles a heavy box of office supplies. Yes, you're officially smitten. Now what?

Before you think about entertaining anything less than platonic, please consider a few things.

1. Are you able to dismiss this as a passing infatuation, or are you convinced that you will be telling stories to your grandchildren someday?

2. Are you drawn to this person because you respect their work ethic? Are you drawn to their status or power? Remember that most people in a position of authority are great candidates for crushes. If this person happens to be your boss or supervisor, FORGET IT unless you are more than willing to leave your job. Don't even go there.

3. Does this person work directly with you in the same department, side by side, day in and day out? Or, do they work for the same company, perhaps on a different floor?

4. Would your future relationship compromise anything for other coworkers? Would it create feelings of discomfort or hostility from others? Would people act weird about it?

5. Does this person frequently date within the company?

Based on those previous questions, let's see how to handle this.

1. If it's a passing attraction - BRAVO! Just enjoy the flirty buzz you get when spending a few extra minutes on your outfit or toothbrushing regiment before running into this person, but please move on to something less dangerous. No harm, no foul!

2. Is it the person or the power? If you aren't sure, just imagine if they came to you dressed as a children's clown. Are you still getting a case of the screaming thighs? If the answer is no, chances are it was your concept of power that made you weaken. Power is undoubtedly one of the ultimate aphrodisiacs, but bedding your boss or supervisor will certainly lead to heartache, and it will end badly. If you are going to go down in flames, choose your power icons well. Are we talking the CEO or head of the firm, or are we talking about the night manager at Crusty Burger? Either way, this tempting little morsel has the power to dismiss you, so don't just throw caution to the wind.

3. If you have daily or constant contact, it may seem wonderful now, but later on reality knocks on your door. "Uh Hi, ... yeah, I'm reality, and I'm here with your check. Would you like to pay me now or later?" Not only do you have to suffer the consequences of working and playing together, but you'll have to endure the eventual exposure

burnout. This is the part where you'd rather claw your eyes out before having to look one more time or laugh at that same tired joke again. Are you willing to endure the angst, discomfort, or the searing pains that shoot through your liver rendering you useless and incapable of making eye contact? Keep reading.

4. Does the object of your affection have a habit of "dipping the pen into the company ink?" If so, you really need to question the motives for this penchant. A career "insider" can only attribute this to laziness, convenience, or opportunistic behavior. Ask yourself if it would really be in your interest to be the next screensaver on his/her laptop.

All right. You caught my subtle axe murderer approach, but before you slam me into the pit of judgment, allow me to explain why I'm handling this with so much enthusiasm. I've seen this lead to heartache and unhappiness with a 98% fatality rate.

On the other hand, if you're one of the lucky 2% who ended up with a soul mate, you are both blessed and lucky. If you're pressing me for sage wisdom about office involvement, I can only warn you that it's usually not your best bet. You'll have to endure gossip, hostilities, discomfort, and the horror of letting your personal life play out in front of the company. Hey! They're just grateful that you've given them something to buzz about. If you are still determined to go for this, I can't stop you, but please may the gods be with you!

♡ ♡ ♡ ♡ ♡ Reader Comments ♡ ♡ ♡ ♡ ♡

Carmen,

I haven't written to you before, but this topic definitley caught my attention! You are right on the money. Been there, done that and I wasn't in the 2%. The first reason was power. I quit my job. The second was STUPIDITY, and I quit my job. I was really hurt, not by the guy, but by my co-workers who really showed their ture colors. They thought I was getting preferential treatment and so on. There was NO company policy stating that we couldn't date, so we did. It honestly started out as friends and MONTHS later did move on to something more, and a year later went on to NOTHING. I admit there were times we displayed our ugly sides in the office. Looking back that wasn't good for anyone. If I am the first to respond to this "issue" let me cheer you on and say I'll have no other part of the office romancing. KEEP UP THE GREAT WORK.

Hi, Carmen,

Let me start by saying I enjoyed this article very much. It hit home. Why? Because that is where I met my best friend who is now my wife. We have worked together for six years. But it took about four before we really became close. So close that we work the same shift, different departments, though. We lunch and break together and are happier now than we have ever been. So as far as being in that 2% bracket, I am terribly happy that we are. Pretty much everything you wrote has happened at work.

How do you know this stuff? Have you been there, done that? Thanks for an interesting article.

♀ Chapter Nine ♂
This Too Shall Pass

Well, it happened. All of those adorable cute things your lover used to do have gone from cute to contemptible. Your shivers of pleasure have turned into cringes of dread, and like rain to a bad hair day, you know it's going to happen. Ending relationships are just a natural part of dating. Shakespeare did not corner the market on painful lament. It is alive and well in the 21st century.

Unfortunately, not all endings are equitable because there's usually a "leaver" and a "leavee." It's rarely pleasant. One either feels jaded, guilty, angry, hurt, miserable or relieved. The writing was on the wall for quite a while. He doesn't remember that he bought you the same gift a year ago, she doesn't attend your softball games anymore, and one of you has taken a new interest in your appearance--for nights when you're not together. The strategy here is not to blame. Blaming is childish. Simply acknowledge the fact that things have changed and not for the greater good.

Remember that every person you date tells you more about what you have to offer in your next relationship. You also have a better grasp of what you would be willing to accept next time and what you would never go through again. Perhaps each ending should be a time of deep reflective closet cleaning. You know what I'm talking about, too. Throw away the things that used to fit but now are too out of style, too big, too small, too raggedy, or just plain unflattering. (I'm not suggesting that you dispose of your partner's things either, so put the scissors down!) The one thing you should remember is that all relationships are learning lessons. Some teach you how to better yourself, and others teach you to enroll in kick boxing, quickly.

Today's Topic: Endings and Beginnings

It's hard to believe that this is already the 50th edition of "Great Sexpectations." I thought it would be appropriate to cover some of the e-mail that I haven't been able to print, either because it was too long or too detailed for the column. What I would like to address are the many letters from my subscribers about how to handle breaking up or separating. For some, a sexual relationship can bring a couple closer together. For others, it can be the factor that ends a union.

Before I run the risk of sounding like "Dear Abby," let me assure you that affairs of the heart are not to be taken lightly. The letters you've sent are proof that some things work in theory, but not in practice. For instance, I could tell you that logically it's time to move forward after a separation, while emotionally you're still nursing a broken heart with no end in sight.

Most of the letters from my subscribers asking for help involve how to get over a relationship. The abrupt ending of a relationship may feel shocking and painful, but it's the person you're missing and not the relationship. For many, the ending of a relationship is considered a failure rather than a learning experience. Why is it a failure? Just because things end, doesn't mean it's a failure. Believe it or not, we come together for many reasons, but the primary function of any union is to learn. Ask yourself, "What did I learn about myself during this relationship? Was my patience tested? Did I become more accepting of myself or others? Did I learn that I have more to offer or give than I ever thought?" These are just a few questions you should ask yourself while you create an emotional checklist.

While it is difficult enough to heal after an ended relationship, some of you share the same group of friends as your "ex" (a term I truly despise). This means you don't have the luxury of physical separation to help you distance yourself from him or her. Keeping that in mind, I can only suggest that you remove yourself (if possible) from the events where you'll have to see this person. This won't be forever, but just long enough to give yourself a breather.

Getting back to the checklist, try to think about all of the positive experiences you shared with this person. Believe it or not, we all learn something new in each relationship. Yes, of course there were negative experiences as well, but those too can be used toward the greater good. "Okay, Carmen, sure..." Before you dismiss this, think about all of your past relationships and what they taught you. Perhaps you dated a smoker before, a control freak, or a lethargic person, etc. By looking to the past, you can now access what your needs will be in the future. Maybe you realized that you could never date another smoker again so you will avoid that in the future. Perhaps you are more comfortable with a passive partner or you'd like to be involved with someone with a large family again.

The point is to use those past relationships to reflect on what you would like to have in the future. Every past relationship tells us more about who we are and what we can bring to a relationship. At this time in my life, I can look back at my previous relationships and define what I would and would not want again. For example, I could never go back to dating anyone too controlling or passive. I now realize what type of personality I'm more comfortable around, and as time passes, you'll also be able to separate from the painful feelings by looking forward to the new ones in your next relationship. For those of you stuck in the "But there will NEVER be anyone like my last love" phase, let me assure you that time handles these feelings as well. No, I'm not suggesting that breaking up is a breeze or a lark, but just like the dung beetles have proven: out of death comes life.

♡ ♡ ♡ ♡ ♡ Reader Comments ♡ ♡ ♡ ♡ ♡

Hello,

I just broke up with my girlfriend of two years yesterday. I was think-ing about it for quite some time, and your topic of breaking up really helped me look at things under a different light. This is my first break up (I'm 20), and I honestly don't know what I'm feeling. I feel like a terrible person, especially after all we've been through. She still wants me back, but in a way, I'm helping both of us. We're in a long distance relationship, and this year I will only be able to see her once every few months for a weekend or so. In the past I have spent the summer with her, but I know that I will not be able to spend time in her city this Christmas or Summer. My friends tell me the bad feeling I'm getting is something I'll get over. I go through different stages of wanting to pull my hair out thinking I still love her and bouts of wanting to have fun and be crazy during my supposedly "prized" college days.

My best friend tells me that if doubts of breaking up have come to mind as strongly as they did, that it was most likely going to happen. I'm still torn apart from this, and I'm not sure if what I'm feeling is the loss of her love or her friendship or if it's something I just need to get over.

Confusedly (for lack of a better ending),
College Loser

[Don't be so hard on yourself. I'm sure you have genuine feelings for her, but realistically, you can't keep life from happening. With your visits so few and far between, it's probably wise to accept the fact that you're both going to meet other people. Try to keep your mind open to new relationships and see how your year shakes out. Your friends are right; the hurt will start to subside in time.]

Today's Topic: Old Boyfriend Part I

Well, I did it! To keep you up to date, I was playing with the idea of looking up my first flame from high school. We were discussing anticipation and excitement that comes with new relationships, so naturally I thought about my first kiss. The more I thought about looking up my old boyfriend, the more intrigued I was. What was he doing? Who did he marry? Did he ever get married? Did he even remember me? Much to my current boyfriend's "delight," I decided to find him!

It all started a few weeks ago after I wrote that column. The idea of Carmen looking up an old boyfriend started a firestorm of controversy with the other Shagmail editors. Fanny encouraged me, but was worried that I would be hurt if he totally forgot me. She turned down the country music and told me that women are much more emotional and attached to their memories. With a glazed look in her eye she asked how I would feel if my ex had changed his name and became a famous professional wrestler who had forgotten his first special girlfriend. Before I knew it, she was running to the bathroom sobbing over some guy named Rock or Triple something!

Next, Chadwick slithered into the room with his usual arsenal of venom ready to verbally eviscerate and sully my schoolgirl memories. Rather than let him ruin my endeavor, I quickly pointed out the group of visiting nuns in our building and watched him dart after them with a grinchly gleam in his eye.

Lewis was the only one who offered any constructive help. He suggested I turn to the Internet to find my long lost paramour, but warned me that this can sometimes get you into trouble with your current partner. He wanted to say more, but then he muttered something about a gag order and returned to his office. TZ wanted me to find my old flame just to see if he had younger sisters who had been in prison.

Mook wanted me to meet with him, but warned me that face to face meetings can often be disappointing. On the other hand it might lead to true romance, so why not? He also made me promise him the exclusive story for his column, no matter how horrible it went.

I finally got the nerve and started searching for him on the Internet. As it turned out, "Troy" still lived near our old high school, so I took a deep breath and wrote to him. Allow me to give you the background. The last time I saw this guy he was the captain of the football and track team, blonde hair, steel blue eyes, blinding smile, and, of course, a frequent volunteer at the local nursing home. Just your average Adonis! At this point you're probably curious about how our meeting went, right? At the risk of pandering to obvious cliff hangers I'll give you a hint: he didn't forget me! I'll spill the details in my next column.

♡ ♡ ♡ ♡ ♡ Reader Comments ♡ ♡ ♡ ♡ ♡

Dear Carmen,

Your e-mail on meeting your high school friend made me laugh, and I really needed to laugh. I always wondered what my Teddy (that was his name) turned out like. I think I'll just try to remember him as the "Italian Stallion," as we called him. I don't think I want to know if he's overweight and bald now with probably three ex-wives.

Dear Carmen,

I, too, wondered after 34 years what had happened to some friends. This past year I set out to find them. One had been married and had kids but had just left a few months before to be with a girl he met on the Internet. I hope he finds happiness. The second one had died of cancer. That was sad. The third one is in prison and has been for many years. I will see this one at Christmas time and let you know how our reunion is. I haven't given up; there are still a couple more to go.

♡ ♡ ♡ ♡ ♡ ♡ ♡ ♡ ♡ ♡ ♡ ♡ ♡ ♡ ♡ ♡ ♡ ♡ ♡

Today's Topic: Old Boyfriend Part II

After deciding to contact my high school sweetheart, I braced myself for what might be an exercise in humiliation. Not only did Troy remember me, HE suggested getting together for coffee to wax nostalgic over the good old days. Pretty harmless, right? Keep reading!

We decided to meet at a local coffee house after work. I warned him that I was 5'10" instead of the 5'5," mouth-full-of-braces gal he left behind. The day arrived with the usual wardrobe trauma that accompanies most reunions, so I grabbed my yearbook and dashed out the door.

I wanted to get there early so I could watch him light up the room with his entrance, but the romance cover model never made his appearance. Instead I was greeted with a beaming red-faced gentleman with a very shiny bald spot and a very hostile female sporting a shiny teamsters jacket. You guessed it. The hostile little woman was his wife who was less than enthused over our meeting (especially when she found out that I wrote a sex column). He extended an awkward handshake and introduced me to his bride, Gloria. Oh, yeah, G-L-O-R-I-A! Let me just say, I was astounded. She was a far cry from the nubile cheerleaders I was used to seeing him with. She was a tough little nugget who (I kid you not) worked at a steel mill. Despite the fact that she had no obvious gender characteristics, I tried to cover my confusion.

Troy had started college on a football scholarship, but it was cut short when he shattered his knee. He dropped out of school and started working for his father's landscaping company. It wasn't the future he had anticipated, but he was happy and doing well. He met Gloria (obviously in her svelte years), and they married. When he produced the family photo of the happy couple and their six kids, I almost fell over. SIX! Prolific little bugger, isn't he?

The meeting went as planned, complete with the awkward moments, pregnant pauses, and nebulous chitchat until Gloria made her way to the "john." As soon as she left, he decided to seize the moment. He started by telling me how great I looked, asked why I wasn't married and offered to finish the kiss I never got at the front door. No sooner did I humor my way out of that idea, when he approached me about some sexual difficulties he was experiencing. My head was spinning! I haven't seen in him in years, and after one cup of coffee he was revealing every problem he and Gloria were having in the bedroom. I thought it was inappropriate to discuss it without Gloria present, but she put my worries to rest as soon as she got back. "Oh, yeah, honey, I asked Troy to run this by you 'cause he ain't cuttin' it in the bedroom anymore!"

It's official: there is a hell, and I'm there now! Gloria told me in her own eloquent way that she does not orgasm with Troy because he's "lame." That was her explanation, and I watched him shrink under the table in abject humiliation. After choking my way through some romantic strategies, I couldn't help feeling sorry for him. I mean between us, Gloria would scare a buzzard off a dung heap, so imagine how his penis felt! After our meeting, I was convinced that his penis had been hiding from her for years and has no intention of coming out of hiding.

I am glad that I can finally put all of my fears to rest. I mean prior to this debacle, I was convinced that he had married a supermodel and lived in a villa somewhere exotic. I think I'll console myself with a glass of wine and snuggle with my present paramour, who is probably grateful that I don't crush walnuts with my thighs or chew tobacco.

♡ ♡ ♡ ♡ ♡ Reader Comments ♡ ♡ ♡ ♡ ♡

Carmen,

I absolutely loved the old boyfriend story! It totally had me in stitches. I might just try it myself.

Dear Carmen,

Reading your last e-mail about your reunion with your younger day sweetheart was great. Glad to see everybody's bride doesn't turn out to be a cheerleader. It sounds like life.

[Nor should every woman be sentenced to life with a football player! Oh, the horror!]

Hey, Carmen,

So SORRY that your high school honey wasn't all that you expected him to be! It kinda sucks that the cute guys in school turn out to be not so cute all grown up, and the not so cute in school turn out to be the hunks all grown up! Well, just like you say, it's done and over with now. You can go on with life! That's one memory you don't have to think about anymore.

[To tell you the truth, I was sort of expecting it. Most of us know what can happen to the early bloomers, right?]

Hi Carmen,

In response to old boyfriends, I'd like to also add that I didn't get to see in person my old flame. Quite a few years back, though, his picture was in our local newspaper. He was getting married, and his wife was NOT what I expected her to look like, but the REAL shocker was, HE didn't look like what I expected him to either.

He had a ring of fuzz around his head and had gained A LOT of weight. I know we all change, so this is not a big deal, but I remembered him because he thought he was SO hot to trot. HA not too Hot to me! Now he resembles the little Caesar pizza guy. Thanks for the hysterical column. Keep up with the good work!

Today's Topic: Make It Stop!

Like the annoying plot of a "B" movie, you hear the bad 70's sound-track music first, followed by the expected "chaa-chaa-chaa" horror sound effects when the unsuspecting babysitter runs out to her car to grab her retainer. Suddenly the music blares, revealing oh, God, I can't look. MERCIFUL HEAVEN! It's her ex-boyfriend whining his way into a superfluous contrived reason for establishing contact, yet again!

From what I've been told, this syndrome is all too common. One half of the now defunct relationship refuses to vanish into the sunset quietly. No sir, not this time. Instead, this person abandons any shred of dignity by random phone calls concerning the oh-so-precious navel lint left behind along with the portion of dental floss that simply must be collected in order to obtain Zen-like harmony.

Let's break this down, shall we? It's what most of us call the "foot in the door" strategy. It usually starts out heavy in the beginning with unexpected visits to claim something of importance (like a comb or toothbrush), but eventually the message is received and contact begins to wane, leading to the desired end, no more contact. Victory is yours, and you no longer have to listen to the whimpering, the groveling, or the plea bargaining to "just be friends."

It sounds cruel, but let's face it; some endings need to be complete, while others can quietly handle occasional contact. It's up to the individual couple to decide the preference, but when a decision has been made, it is in the best interest of both parties to stick to the agreement. When one insists on continual contact, it can only lead to hostility and complete annoyance. Some defy good sense by attempting the stalking approach. This features more than one phone call or surprise visit; it usually comes in the manic form of 10-15 phone calls in one evening plus a few extras scattered around to some of your friends for good measure. The only thing sealed is your utter contempt for the obvious disregard of your wishes.

The next scenario is much more passive-aggressive. This time it involves one of the walking wounded who no longer tries to establish contact, but makes it a point to engage you in a public place using some untoward attention-getting behavior. This over-grown child takes his or her pouting into polite society by pulling out an arsenal of bad behavior. The most common is the dirty look. This staring becomes so pervasive that everyone in eye shot takes a preemptive step towards the door before things get thrown. If staring doesn't yield the desired results, perhaps a round of jukebox terrorism would get the desired attention. This trick involves a hostile takeover of the jukebox whereby the wounded party feeds $1,000 in quarters into the machine and chooses only the poignant tunes designed to belittle you. There's nothing subtle about the title choices:

3 Doors Down - "Loser"
Nine Inch Nails - Anything from *The Downward Spiral*
Disturbed - "Stupefied"
The Smiths - "How Soon is Now?"
Back - "I'm a Loser" (see a pattern here?)
The Cure - "Funeral"

You get the idea, right? There is, of course, the really severe form of jukebox terrorism--playing the same song 100 times in a row to make sure the point is driven home or you're driven into the night.

If all of this has a familiar ring (I can't wait to get this batch of e-mail), just consider how foolish these tactics are. Not only does this give dating a bad name, the interrogator usually winds up looking like a real fool. Don't give in to your desperate need to have the last word. Exercise a little dignity and class. At least you can hold your head up in polite society knowing that you took the high road.

♡ ♡ ♡ ♡ ♡ Reader Comments ♡ ♡ ♡ ♡ ♡

Hi, Carmen!

I have been going through this for two years now! It's GREAT to know there are other people out there that notice. Actually, I'm not the target. My boyfriend had an ex-girlfriend and an ex-wife (separated two years and still coming back) that would keep calling! The ex girl-friend would drop by about once a month. Finally it died down to where we were only getting about one call from each a month, then one call every two months.

But every time one of them called, they always had something they left here or something they had of my boyfriend's. It's always something!

There were even two occasions where we ran into his psycho ex-girl-friend, and, yes, there was some jukebox terrorism. But, she played loving songs (country bar, get the hint?). Or "I miss you" songs. It got ugly that night. But she still calls on holidays! You would think that after two years of LEAVE ME ALONE she would get on with her life. I'm in my late 20's, but this makes me feel like a teenager! Anyway, I just wanted to say thanks for that article. I passed it on to my boyfriend, and he thought it was great. He finally woke up and realized it's not good to talk to the psycho ex one time and tell them to go away the next. You do one or the other!

Dear Carmen,

I wanted to comment on your last issue. I agree that those tactics are stupid and foolish. My ex pulled the stalker approach. He would call my house and hang up, e-mail me constantly, show up at my house and at my school and threaten to ruin my life. I finally obtained a trespassing order, and he still showed up at my house. He even called my current boyfriend and told him all kinds of horrible things. I don't understand why people do this; it's foolish and very cruel.

Carmen,

You are so right about these losers who can't let go when a relationship is over. Unfortunately, I have been unlucky enough to have these sorts of scenarios from three different guys in the past, and every one has made my life a misery. I am sure that the idea behind ringing 25 times per night crying on the phone or telling you how dreadful you are for leaving such a "catch" is more to do with hurting and revenge though, than any sort of logical "I want you back" behavior. No matter what I said or did, none of these guys would take the hint, even when I got the police involved. In the end the only way I could get away was to physically move where they couldn't find me. Drastic, I know, but sometimes it's the only way to make it stop and keep your own sanity!

Carmen,

My former spouse drives past my house on a routine basis. (He doesn't exercise his visitation rights.) Being a single mother I only get to go out once in awhile. So I choose my time carefully. When and if I go, I like to stop by the local watering hole for a beer and a game of pool, only to have him show up and do the inevitable stare down, leading to the get drunk and make an a** of himself. So I have to drive to the next town about 50 miles. The worst part of this is that he has remarried. Needless to say that any man I date usually gets to see firsthand the things I put up with. However, this also makes for a lot of first dates.

♀ Chapter Ten ♂

Mixed Nuts

The beauty of relationships is that so much of what we do defies classification and logic for that matter! Explain flirting or fetishes in a scientific matter? Not likely. What about voyeurism or fantasies? What fascinates us are the similarities; what intrigues us are the differences. If I had a dime for every letter that ended with the phrase, "...is this normal?" I would be rich. Never has one subject been the cause for so much insecurity or alarm. Sex is an equal opportunity provider of doubt. It's perfectly understandable, too.

Think about any other activity that leaves us feeling so vulnerable, exposed, or possibly humiliated. Now, multiply it by 1,000. Aside from trying on bikinis under fluorescent lighting after a huge meal, I cannot think of anything else more rife with angst.

My favorite part of this job is the reader mail. Everyone has their own unique spin to contribute, especially when it comes to reflections about sex and romance--which, by the way, do not always go hand in hand. Yes, I even covered the gratification bandits who attract, conquer, and leave before you can blink an eye.

Consider this a quilting chapter where every column fits together here, just not everywhere else! This quilt of sorts covers everything from rage and revenge sex to the bar and club scenes. The green-eyed monster makes an appearance, along with several topics that inspired a flurry of responses like "Healing Hurts" and "Personality or IQ."

Today's Topic: Defining the Bar Scene: Part I

As we continue to uncover the naked truth about human sexuality, it has become apparent (via e-mail requests) that I should discuss the often feared, often avoided, and much maligned bar scene. People have written to me about relationships, but the one comment that never gets explained is the one that goes, "...And I'm so NOT doing the bar thing again!" That just screams negative experience, so I thought I'd get a professional perspective on the whole issue and hopefully clear the air.

I was recently given a valuable opportunity to interview a friend and neighbor who co-owns a neighborhood hot spot. This man is more credible than most of the so-called experts for one simple reason: this is his livelihood, and he sees EVERYTHING from a bird's eye view. Not only does he get to be the fly on the wall, but he gets to orchestrate some of the activity in an oh-so-subtle way.

Before I start, let me define what I mean by a bar. This particular place happens to be a bar, but it's also a restaurant, pool hall, and gaming area type wing-ding with a stone fireplace, wood floors, and a sprinkling of wildlife lithographs on the walls. In other words, it's not a 20-seat straight bar tavern, nor is it a dance club. The ethos in a dance club is not even the same animal; those places and the pervasive behavior will be discussed at length next week. Be brave, it's not for the faint of heart.

My first question was pretty basic: "Why do people come to a place like this?" The answer is not to pick up a warm body; that's too dismissive and too easy. To be precise, we're all quite social, and most of us thrive on human contact. If you consider the 40-50 hour work week mixed in with the odd hours spent running errands, paying bills, and ironing the cat, there's not much left. In the interest of fighting cabin fever or staving off "afghan syndrome" as my friend calls it, we put forth the effort to comb hair, brush teeth, and join the human race. Or do we? It seems that many people find the whole task too daunting. Fear and insecurity keep many of us at home because there's this perceived stigma attached to an outing at a public house.

Most of the fear surrounds the perception of our arrival. Why is he or she here? What are they looking for? Is he or she alone or traveling with a group of friends? There must be some agenda, right? Slow down. You're giving it too much thought. Sometimes people just want a friendly atmosphere and polite conversation. Or they might be looking to meet someone new. Before assigning any tawdry insights, I'll explain the ground rules as I was instructed.

If you happen to be female and you're alone or with one girlfriend, the proprietor or greeter will generally try to seat you at the bar instead of a table. Simply put, it's easier to make conversation around a bar than it is if you separate yourself from the crowd. This particular establishment was designed with a circular bar so the patrons could see everyone. If you're at a well-run establishment, the bartender will be prompt and polite without acting too busy or curt. A bartender with a poor demeanor sets the tone of the place, and if they treat you like a second class citizen, you're not likely to stay long or return.

You'll notice that part one of this missive centers on female behavior. Not to fret--men are equally important, but I was told that how women behave will then determine what the men do, so please be patient. The women/woman will be observed at various stages of her visit, but here's the tricky part: all body language will be intensely observed for further cues. If she/they decide(s) to sit at the bar, they will be observed by the way they sit, hold a drink, and most of all--if they make eye contact. Not just any old eye contact, but the eye contact followed by a smile. This DOES NOT mean she's "lookin' fir it." It simply means that she's friendly and will welcome conversation.

Most men will continue to wait after the smile for further study of her body language. Is she sitting with her arms or legs crossed? Perhaps she's just comfortable, so I was told the one action to pay very close attention to. I can't believe I'm writing this, but it boils down to how she plays with her hair, tilts her neck, and loosens her shoulders. I was told that the more she plays with her hair or exposes her neck, the more approachable she is. Generally the more animated, the better it is for a nervous stranger to approach. (I was also told that this generally begins after the second drink.)

It sounds too simple, doesn't it? Well, if you've watched bird behavior on National Geographic, I'm told that this similar kind of preening is also quite effective in the wild. This is by no means an admonishment; it's actually quite refreshing to know that there is some inherent genetic coding at work. It's also a relief to know that subconscious behavior can sometimes save ourselves from ourselves. What I mean is that some women enter the arena with a caustic attitude, and it shows. If you have a hostile aura or a chip on your shoulder, only a fool would try to approach you so it's okay to smile...you're not a slut!

The ensuing animation is much like the first only she gets more aggressive until (I'm told) she actually tilts her head and exposes an ear. According to my sage, the ear exposure happens after the initial ice breaker and after the conversation is deemed more than suitable. This ear thing supposedly means not only is there interest, but most certainly sexual interest/arousal. Kinda makes you think about your earrings doesn't it?

As an aside, I'd like to be the first to point out that the Emperor has no clothes, i.e. if you really hate human contact and want total solitude, you would have stayed at home in your grungy sweats. Let's call a spade a spade. On the other side, contact could simply mean company and not a "Love Connection." I'm tired of bars getting the bad rap when the bad rap is truly perpetuated by social oafs.

Part two covers male behavior, good and bad, which night out means what and hopefully offering some basic guidelines for your next endeavor. Mind you this is just one man's offerings, but I went out twice after our interview just to prove him wrong, and I could not. Everything he said was spot-on correct. That includes the group of women who go out to relieve job stress. Being in a group makes it harder, but your smile will travel beyond your table. Tune in next column so I can share what I was told about men. (Being female only gives you so much insight.)

♡ ♡ ♡ ♡ ♡ Reader Comments ♡ ♡ ♡ ♡ ♡

Dear Carmen,

Carmen, you rock! I work at a night club in Los Angeles. Different nights of the week we host different promotions (DJs and music, not drink specials). Here are a few tips for people to enjoy themselves:

Pretend you're someone else. Decide you're an outgoing person and do it. The easiest way is if you catch someone looking at you twice-- SMILE and say HI! You can even tell them that's why you said "hi." (This goes for guys and girls.)

Take a cab or have someone responsible drive. Don't feed them shots. Say "hi" to the doorperson. He needs a friendly gesture, as crowd control sucks. Offer to bring him a Coke or water. Generally they won't accept, but they'll remember you. Talk to the bouncers. Ladies, they are your saviors, and guys, they'll kick the other guy out. Be nice to your bartender (me) when the crowd is five deep. It's hard to know exactly who's next. We remember tippers. I know drinks are expensive, but we don't see any of that money. All we see is the tip. My paycheck for two weeks work is usually around $50.00. If you're paying with a credit card, slip the bartender a five after a couple rounds. It's worth it to see them jump over the bar just to serve you.

When trying to get through a crowd, gently put your hand on someone's shoulder or arm and say something cute like "Love ya, can I squeeze by?" "Excuse me, Doll" and more, whatever works or what you feel comfortable saying. P.S. I'm female. Say something even if you don't think they can hear you. Club people hear everything.

The friendlier you are the more likely you'll find people to surround you. They'll buy you drinks, make sure you're invited into the VIP room, and much more can happen. This will come from either the same sex or opposite. (Same sex doesn't mean they want you in that way.)

I go to clubs to have fun, not to hook up. Most regulars are the same. I'll run into someone who's fun, and I keep in contact with them through the night. If they have more club experience, generally they're buying the drinks and walking me into VIP and introducing me to the people they know. (Let them buy you drinks. Chances are they aren't paying full price, but always offer a round or two.) If it's "my club," it's my turn. Always remember to reciprocate courtesy.

Remember to walk with a big smile. People don't smile enough in clubs. It's much cooler to walk around and see who's looking at you. I've found that to be utter BULLSH*T. By smiling, people will smile back. It's hard not to. Again, say "hi." People who are "in the scene" need to find people they can enjoy hanging with. If you enjoy yourself, others will enjoy you, too.

Carmen, feel free to edit. Have a fabulously fun day!

♡ ♡ ♡ ♡ ♡ ♡ ♡ ♡ ♡ ♡ ♡ ♡ ♡ ♡ ♡ ♡ ♡ ♡ ♡ ♡

Today's Topic: The Bar Scene: Part II

Last issue we covered some basic guidelines about how women are watched at a bar/restaurant. So this week I'll try to cover the rather extensive list of what men are watching, thinking, or perhaps doing. There are no blanket answers or statements, so read this with a big grain of salt and an open mind.

My interview with the bar owner (sorry, Anne Rice) was a real mixed experience. I found myself sitting with that "tell me something I don't know" attitude which I quickly replaced with a "wow, you're kidding, right?" attitude. Like most of you, I'd like to think that common sense prevails when it comes to human behavior, but I'm sure I would be side-lined by any psychologist worth his/her salt if I tried to reduce human behavior in a few paragraphs. For the record, I wrote about the interview for fun and to share something that I found helpful and intriguing.

For the men I've never met before, I owe you an apology for underestimating how much you go through in the quest to just say "hello." Most innocent men are paying the price for the egomaniacs who have approached women with the warehouse club mentality, i.e. "flirt in bulk." It saves time and money. For every man out there who has tried, or worse, not tried to approach a woman out of fear, this is for you.

God help the man who is genuinely attracted to a woman who must overcome years of bad press by introducing himself. It's no wonder that they wait until they've had a few drinks (or more) until they approach the "mountain." Like women there is doubt and insecurity, but if you read the last issue, you should study her body language and follow the golden rule--her smile, that is. At no time in history has anyone flashed a warm smile at a stranger that revolts them, so first, follow your instincts. Try not to look too nervous and avoid the two biggest mistakes (according to my guru) which are:

1. Do not violate her personal space bubble too soon. Americans by culture have a wider area of personal space whereas in another country, you can speak very closely to a person's face without a reaction. As a rule, most of us feel comfortable with a good 18-26 inches between body parts. If you get too close, she'll react instantly. She'll cross her legs or her arms, cover her neck or actually shrink back. (there's a red hot clue, huh?)

Sometimes men will get too close without realizing that it sets up an environment of discomfort. Let her move towards you. If the music is too loud and she gets really close to your ear, let her continue until you get the signal that you can get close to her ear. Usually she will place it right in front of your mouth so she can hear you. It's up to you to decide if it's just a volume control issue or a good excuse to get close.

2. The second big error men make is grasping for an opening line. Huge, huge error according to my sage. No woman wants to feel like she's being pitched to like so much bad advertising. Along with the opening line (this is twofold) comes the "traveling salesman" enigma. If you've been pollinating every woman at the bar with your honey tongue, give it up. No woman in the world wants to be part of your fishing net technique of socializing. The girls ARE watching, they just don't let you see them, and if you've decided to rifle through the bar like a S.W.A.T. leader... you know where this is going.

Back to the opening line. I asked what was the right thing to say and was stunned by the elegance and simplicity of this answer. He said, "Just introduce yourself" as in, "Hi, my name is..." I was dumbfounded because I don't remember anyone approaching me with this novel idea. Amazing, but I thought about how I would react to a man that just politely offered his name--floored! What a concept! Nothing sordid or tawdry, no fishing for vapid compliments, just a name. The genius lies in the simplicity. Can you think of anything more refreshing?

Obviously, this had a great impact on my perception of the male gender, and now I'm just waiting with bated breath (mental note to self: look up bated breath) for a stranger to just...introduce himself. Aaahhhh, simple pleasures. Of course women would find a whole new world if they did the introduction or approach first, but most will not make the first move for fear of looking too aggressive.

I promised I would give the day of the week analogy which won't come as any surprise, but for those unaware, here's the scoop:

Monday - a great day to gather and socialize provided it's Monday Night Football season. Otherwise it's rather slow.

Tuesday, Wednesday - This is usually when groups of coworkers going out to detox from the day. Perhaps a great day to meet the newest desk rage candidate.

Thursday - perhaps the most mysterious night of the week. During the interview I asked the usual question of why? It's still a work night, and you have to get up early the next day, so why is it so popular? The only answer I got was a genuine confusion but the term was, "it's animal on Thursdays like there was a full moon in the parking lot. All bets are off on Thursdays, and anything can happen." Frightening words because even he looked nervous while mentally recounting Thursdays at his bar. Exciting? Yes. Daunting? You bet. Take your chances, my friends.

Friday, Saturday - Forget date night out. Both nights the crowd is more numerous, more relaxed and genuinely friendly. As an aside, the word "friendly "was definitely not used in the Thursday description. In my estimation, it would be the best time to go because it's crowded enough to provide a little comfort and coverage.

Sunday - usually a sporting enthusiast crowd, but still on the friendly side. Sundays are usually more laid back, and you're less apt to find the "Christina or Britney" look-alikes clad in something purely MTV.

As a recap these are the highlights: Girls, smile and let your hair down if you're interested. Most of all don't punish a man for trying. If you think it's so easy, you approach first. Men, don't use an opening line. Try introducing yourself in a straight forward fashion. Make sure you don't violate the personal space bubble too soon, either.

My deepest thanks to my friend, neighbor and sage. Please have fun with the bar scene observations and feel free to share your advice for me to print soon. These are just ideas and not the gospel, so go easy on the criticisms in your letters. In closing, I'd like to tell you that I really did go out to try to disprove his theories, but alas, it all held water!

♡ ♡ ♡ ♡ ♡ Reader Comments ♡ ♡ ♡ ♡ ♡

Dear Carmen,

I know that where I live in NY Thursday nights are when all the local bands play at all the local bars/taverns/and small dance clubs. Thursday nights are for some people the end of the work week, with some companies having flex Fridays. It is the night where you can have a girl/boys night out, and you get to see friends if you know that you won't see them on the weekend.

I know being the only single person in my group of friends that I only really see them on Thursday nights because the weekends are reserved for their boyfriends/girlfriends. I hope this has helped your "why do so many people go out on Thursday night" question.

Today's Topic: Dance Clubs Part I

Last week we braved the topic of the "bar scene" thanks in large part to my friend and neighbor who granted me an interview about bar behavior. While I tried to deliver the information in an unbiased fashion, I promised to discuss the other side of the bar scene which is the slightly more aggressive dance club. Without being judgmental or maligning this institution, I thought it only fair to cover this venue of sometimes social mayhem.

If you thought the bar scene was not a valid place to meet somebody of the opposite sex, the dance clubs should be left to seasoned veterans with implacable emotional armor and self-esteem covered in flubber. Allow me to explain.

Dance clubs for the most part are designed to be spacious, flashy, loud, distracting, and for the most part, austere. Most do not elicit a feeling of warmth or comfort. They are meant to serve massive amounts of people by catering to every need from video games to sports. These clubs are small cities held together by loud dance music and a carnival-like atmosphere.

You'll also notice that the more gigantic places come complete with a small army of security guards equipped with uniforms, walkie-talkies, and a demeanor fit for war games. I don't know if any of you see it the same way, but am I wrong for not feeling enveloped in comfort or friendliness?

I know what you're thinking, and you're quite right. I enjoy visiting these places every once in a while so I can just disappear into the music and people watch. Dance clubs offer enough atmosphere for one to simply disappear into, but I am addressing the practice of meeting people in these establishments. Considering the scope inside, it's no wonder that crowds match their demeanor to the place. You'll find that the more expansive or fantastic the club, the more outrageous the attire gets. Men and women alike tend to travel by wolf pack, but it seems as if all behavior is amended accordingly. Women who are really more comfortable in their favorite jeans will suddenly take to wearing MTV fashions with little imagination and even less material. After donning their flimsiest outfit, they will then roll their eyeballs and complain about how rude the men are who gape and ogle them.

I smell a mixed message here, don't you? For future reference, please visit any ladies room and listen to the ensuing complaints as they apply more lip gloss and head back to the trenches for fun. In addition to the wardrobe choices you'll also notice the "sparkle plenty" makeup. In keeping with the theme of post-nuclear fallout/industrial destruction, some ladies have taken to glitter, lots of it.

I love Halloween but let's call a spade a spade. One of the reasons dance clubs exist is so people can assume a different identity for fun. No harm here, but if you're going there to find Mr. or Ms. Perfect, you might want to adjust your sights.

I'll probably get a flood of e-mail about how many of you hooked up with your current honey at "Defcon 5," but I'm trying to focus on the majority. No, it's not easy to meet people here based on volume alone, but if you actually visit one of these places to play "fly on the wall," you'd be amazed at how blatant the behavior is matched only by how rude it can be.

I'll start this two-part observation by sharing my experience with a particular group of males who were quite obviously looking for hot and heavy female companionship for about 12 minutes. Enter the "safety in numbers" group. All are dressed accordingly with only one wearing more chains than Marley's ghost. After I regained consciousness from the crop dusting of Polo, Cool Water, and Envy, I witnessed a seek- and-destroy mission that would have impressed Charles Bronson. Not only did they center themselves at the one table that overlooks the front door, they didn't even have the decency to feign conversation amongst the group.

Not this crew. They perched themselves with vulture-like precision that would of course enable them to see every patron upon entrance, thereby eliminating the need to mingle. It was with this time-saving endeavor that kind of made my blood run cold. Their facial expressions were no less obvious than Caesar's thumbs up or down motion at a gladiator event. Chilling it was.

(Yes, I'm having fun with this, but I am writing for your entertainment as well as making a point.) My continued observation of the said group did not bode well for the rest of civilization. They displayed a frightening amount of arrogance which was either fear or the adrenaline rush still surging through their veins from the gym. One was visible checking out his own pectorals, but that's a story for another day.

I simply must disclose the rest of the evening, but I'll share the rest in part two of the dance club endeavor. Chiding as I may sound, I really do love visiting these places to get lost in the music, but is it wrong for a gal with a fertile imagination to amuse herself in the process? I say no! Stay tuned for my next edition where I'll disclose the rest of the events and try to offer some constructive advice as well.

♡ ♡ ♡ ♡ ♡ Reader Comments ♡ ♡ ♡ ♡ ♡

Hey, Carmen,

Are you Ann Landers?

[Good God, no!]

Carmen,

Much of what you state about clubs is unfortunately true. I have first-hand experience since I work in the industry as a theme producer and promoter. Much of the mainstream culture is overbearingly obnoxious and very illiterate as to what a club is intended for. Most clubbers go in hope that they will be the center of attention or that they should be there so they can say that they are part of the "in" crowd, whatever that means.

After a while, most clubs are boring because these people do not know how to have a good time on there own, always expecting a club to provide for them, no matter what the events call for. And to a point, clubs are supposed to provide the good time, but because these people go to these clubs every Thursday, Friday and Saturday night, they can't possibly expect to be entertained all the time. They go in expecting a whole new ball game when they were there less than 24 hours prior!

The people who have a good time are the ones who can take a club for what it's worth. They aren't necessarily there to score a piece of ass; they are there so they can get away from the everyday bullsh*t life has to offer. It's a place that provides the backdrop for an evening to dance, drink, and socialize with whom they feel comfortable. The ones who take the clubs at face value will always have the most fun.

Most people I associate with go in order to dance there ass off in a musical experience. Not to act like a jerk to try and be cool. The coolest people you can associate yourself with in a club are the people that SMILE, SMILE, DANCE, and actually say "excuse me." If people could remember to be more polite and a little gracious, the overall experience would be much nicer.

♡ ♡ ♡ ♡ ♡ ♡ ♡ ♡ ♡ ♡ ♡ ♡ ♡ ♡ ♡ ♡ ♡ ♡ ♡ ♡

Today's Topic: Dance Clubs Part II

Last time we were discussing the differences between the bar scene and the dance club scene, which are two very separate experiences. While I don't rule out meeting interesting people, I will suggest exercising caution and try to cover a few rules of survival. As I mentioned earlier, dance clubs are large and austere with the express purpose of serving large crowds while providing sensory overload. If you're like me, you probably enjoy listening to the music, but you're not there to involve yourself in much conversation.

According to those in the know (I interviewed an industry magnet and full time hipster who calls himself Sri), these are the guidelines with which you'll need to equip yourself for the industrial endeavor:

1. Nothing happens before midnight. Apparently it lies deep in the ten commandments somewhere that thou shalt not appear before 12:00 a.m. for fear that one might look too anxious or too gainfully employed. It also tells the novices in the crowd that anything worth doing can be done in two hours or less.

2. If the club is not packed shoulder to shoulder, it's not worth your time. You are paying $8 per cocktail (when you finally squeeze your way to the bar) just to risk spilling it or having your new friends tap an ash into it. It goes along with the old "anything THIS crowded has to be GREAT" school of thinking. It also entices those who feel that many bodies will only maximize their chances of meeting somebody.

3. When choosing a dance club, stay away from the tourist traps. Any club that advertises during the Superbowl is probably a corporate tourist trap. If you really want to know where to go, ask a local bartender. He knows where everyone goes because he has to go somewhere when he gets off work at 1:00 a.m. Because he is an industry

person, he can tell you where these obscure dens of hipness reside. He'll also give you the heads up on who has the cool VIP rooms and how you'll have no chance of seeing one.

4. Think Thursday. Again, I have not yet heard a decent explanation about why this is such a hot night, but I was told that many prefer to go out on Thursdays to avoid the influx of tourists or suburbanites.

5. If you want to avoid the long pretentious lines outside of your favorite spot, try something really radical. I was told you could call the club during office hours (9-5) and ask the club to reserve you and your party some space for later that week. Really.

6. Fashion advice. Don't wear the latest style if it's not flattering on you. I saw many women squeezing into the Jennifer Lopez just-barely-there fashions, which sounds great unless you're built like the Staypuff Marshmallow Man. Even women with fabulous figures can wear something that is totally unflattering. Ask a friend what they think, and if *you're* the friend--be honest. When in doubt, wear black.

7. You're in a dance club. Dance! Nobody expects you to perform Riverdance. Just relax and have fun on the dance floor. One of the greatest things about dance clubs is that you don't have to have a partner. Grab some floor and join the masses. You might find it's easier to talk to a stranger if you're both dancing in the same area. If you do strike up a conversation with someone, offer to buy them a drink while you catch your breath. Logical and polite--what a combination.

8. If you're a shy man you might want to go with a group of female friends. This way you can dance with them without any pressure, and after you loosen up, you might be more inclined to talk or dance with someone else. If you're alone and a man, sit at the bar and try to look comfortable and friendly. If you look distant or uptight, you will remain alone, distant, and uptight.

9. Women should also remain aware while on the dance floor. Because it's crowded and dancing entails some rather obvious bump and grind motions, it has the potential to get ugly. If you know how loud the music is, it should come as no surprise that nobody will hear you scream. Women have literally been molested on the dance floor mere inches away from other people without being noticed.

10. Part of the allure these clubs try to promote is what I like to call the "freak show factor." These places thrive on the outrageous and the uncommon, so be prepared to see open drug use, sexually overt behavior, unisex bathrooms (even if they really aren't), or a melange of semi-conscious spaced-out automatons with no perceptible manners.

It's not a slam; it's just a realistic glimpse of what to expect. You can have a really great time, but if you have no idea what these places are like, it can get in the way of the fun factor. I've seen some people incredulous over the experience while others embrace it because it's not on the beaten path. I wouldn't suggest going if you're already a bastion of insecurity. The crowd can be edgy and aggressive which might put some people off. If you can go without worrying about what others think, you'll be much better off. So much for the club scene. You are encouraged to write about your experiences so we can sort through them together. Remember that variety is the spice of life, and any learning experience is valid. Don't avoid trying new things out of fear because you might miss out!

♡ ♡ ♡ ♡ ♡ Reader Comments ♡ ♡ ♡ ♡ ♡

Hi, Carmen:

Just thought I would share with you that in San Diego (my home) a lot of bars and clubs have Girls Night Out on Thursdays. They will offer half-price drinks and/or free cover charge to all girls. This is a way to encourage both sexes to go out on what would ordinarily be a slow night. If the girls are there, the boys will be, too! By the way, my girlfriends and I always had a rule:

We go out together,
We go home together,
No extra passengers...

You break the rule, you aren't invited next time! This really kept us safe. We always watched out for each other, but we were still able to drink, dance, and flirt! If one of the girls is insistent on taking a guy home with her, tell her that she could give him directions to her house and he could meet her there, but no extra passengers are allowed, and she must ride home with us.

[Safety first, my friends!]

Carmen,

You hit the proverbial "nail on the head" with the dance club scene. However, just to point out, your "when in doubt go black" comment is great, but if you are going to a dance club with black lights, you better make sure to attack your clothes with a lint brush before you go! Even if you can't see it in the light of your home, it'll be there when you walk into the black light. Also, you didn't state this, and it may be an extremely obvious suggestion, but girls... GO IN GROUPS!

Whether it's to the club, leaving the club, or even to the bathroom. It may make men feel like you are "unapproachable," but safety is a big issue in these places and, I'd much rather worry about that than making it a little hard for a guy to talk to me. If he's interested enough he'll approach me anyway, or I'll just approach him! Thanks for all the great advice, Carmen. Keep it coming!

♡ ♡ ♡ ♡ ♡ ♡ ♡ ♡ ♡ ♡ ♡ ♡ ♡ ♡ ♡ ♡ ♡ ♡ ♡

Today's Topic: Rage Sex

Sometimes I like to stir things up by discussing things that don't always appear in books or polite conversation; that's just human nature. Last night I found myself immersed in a highly provocative subject: rage sex. That's not the universally understood technical term, but it works for me. I'm curious about how many of my readers are familiar with this practice.

It's like road rage for the bedroom. I say this because it can happen without warning complete with skid marks, primal screams, and unannounced lane changes. Most of you know this as "angry sex," which it is, but rage sex takes it one step further. Before you dash off an e-mail to me about sex and violence, don't. I'm not in any way endorsing physical harm or domestic abuse. Rage sex is consensual, and it usually follows a heated argument.

Some of you have expressed confusion about this phenomenon because it flies in the face of reason that two people would desire intimacy after hurt feelings, anger, or lack of closure. As the song goes, it's a thin line between love and hate. This is the premise behind rage sex. When a couple connects sexually, it's the most intense form of nonverbal communication (no offense to any career mimes).

Most of us have vulnerability issues that we don't easily vocalize. The unspoken fears, unfulfilled desires, or the deep disappointments that we've buried can be addressed through body language. For example, if you feel intimidated or uncomfortable in a room filled with strangers, you will most likely stand with your arms folded or your legs crossed. This position tells everyone that you are not comfortable or easy to approach. Intimacy is a physical surrender that gives your partner unlimited access to your deepest feelings. When we make love we communicate volumes to our partners through raw vocal and physical validation. Every moan, gasp, shiver, and embrace is a visceral expression of unbridled desire or passion. It's this kind of passion that we find most difficult to talk about. As I have been told repeatedly, "I can do it without a problem, but don't ask me to talk about it." Enter rage sex.

You and your partner have silently acknowledged friction within the relationship. Perhaps one has become incommunicative and the other is seeking clarity, an understanding, or answers to questions that were continually avoided. Most of us have been with partners who avoid confrontation, but when the Cheese Whiz finally hits the fan, the argument takes a drastic turn. What begins as a constructive conversation or a venting session ends in a frenzy of pure emotion.

What we can't articulate in words we can often demonstrate physically. Rage sex is not about having sex while angry; it's the culmination and climax of aggravation, passion, lust, and power in one very explosive sexual endeavor. I am sure some of you have experienced this and just did not know what to call it. Does it sound familiar?

As destructive as it sounds, it serves as an extreme relief for tension, and the level of intensity often rekindles a buried passion which most of us thrive on. Rage sex acts as a catalyst to assuage frustration. To be precise, it purges our feelings and cleanses the soul. Couples usually experience a closer bond because it's so volatile. I don't mean that it repairs every relationship. It usually takes place between two people who share more than just a sexual interest. It's the stuff that keeps our souls intact and reminds us that we are very much alive.

If you are the type that avoids anger or confrontation, you might want to possibly rethink your strategy. Actions almost always speak louder than words. Stay off the highway and think about redirecting your anger in a more positive fashion.

♡ ♡ ♡ ♡ ♡ Reader Comments ♡ ♡ ♡ ♡ ♡

Dear Carmen,

Thanks for the advice on rage sex. It fully explains what I went through with this one guy. I wasn't quite sure what had happend until I read your newsletter. I knew things weren't right, before, during and after it happened. He had shown this new interest in me, and I wasn't sure what to make of it. Now I know what to look out for. Thanks!

Today's Topic: Revenge Sex

I knew it was only a matter of time before the masses retaliated. Apparently the column on rage sex was so well received that my astute readers identified a more specific category of sex. Let us now explore your topic: revenge sex.

It goes without saying that I'm not here to condone, promote, reject, or persuade any aspect of human sexuality. However, there's always a handful of readers who write to me in anger spewing their disapproval over the subject matter. The topic of sex entails all aspects, pleasant and unsavory. I'm trying to give a voice to the things that are only whispered about so we can address them in the light of day, together.

I agree that the transition between rage sex and revenge sex was a natural progression, and many of you wanted to discuss the differences. First, remember that most behavior behind closed doors happens in the moment, without premeditation.

For the most part, this column presents subjects that call for planning. This time I'd like to focus on something that might not be pleasant, but if you can identify the signs, it can be avoided.

Several of my readers have shared some painful stories about how they were used as a revenge token in someone else's game. It's never a pleasant realization, but there are a few warning signs to which you may fall victim.

In the first scenario, the angry or hurt partner is actively seeking revenge sex to retaliate or get back at their lover. This person is easy to identify because they will generally pursue you fast and hard. They will slather you with attention and aggressively pursue a sexual endeavor very early in the relationship. It's easy to sense this agenda because it doesn't follow a natural rhythm. Hence your first clue that it's been planned. If it actually gets to the point where you've decided to pursue sex, ask yourself if it feels forced, or if you've been pressured. If the answer is yes, rethink your decision.

The second type of predator is someone on a longer mission. What I mean is this person has been hurt so badly that they approach relationships with a defense strategy. They will indirectly punish the son for the sins of the father or the daughter for the sins of the mother. This person decided that all men/women are defective, and it is their express duty to hurt them in the name of every man or woman who has suffered a romantic injustice. They tend to be defensive, emotionally closed, and expect you to expose your vulnerabilities without sharing any of their own. This one is harder to detect, but when it comes to sex, they can either be too eager or suspiciously uninterested. While their demeanor may be pleasant, pay close attention to what ISN'T being said. Most people who fall victim to this are also the type who see only what they want to see. Remember my favorite expression by Maya Angelou? "When people show you who they are, believe them."

Before I close let me try to explain something on behalf of those predators. I chose the word to stress a point, but I'm certainly not saying that they victimize on purpose. We all entertain a darker side, and most humans are masters of rationalization. We figure, "I won't be the first or the last, so what harm could it really do?" It's an empty gesture that doesn't even any score. It's a waste to put forth the effort while secretly damning your ex with every thrust and scratch. If the philosophy behind your actions is to "get them before they get me," you need to ask yourself some serious questions. It's an empty gesture that can and should be avoided. Until next time, don't drive or date angry.

 Reader Comments

Hello,

Very interesting article, Carmen. Whenever I think about revenge I remember a quote I heard, I belive by Gandhi, "When you seek revenge, you allow the person to hurt you more." Just my two cents.

Dear Carmen,

I read this with increasing shock. This is my ex-husband! It wasn't sex that split us up, though. He did some terrible things in other areas of his life, but it was only after I decided to leave him after nine years of marriage, that I finally was able to see his disinterest in the bedroom--after an initial passionate pursuit--as having been his way of manipulating and punishing me. What a revelation that there's actually a name for it!

Carmen,

I want to thank you for the warning about revenge sex. I can relate to the first scenario, and I think that reading your description has identified something for me to avoid. I have recently been hurt very badly by my wife (she had an affair, and I found out in a very traumatic fashion), and I have just realized that I've been entertaining the notion of having my own, to "even out the score." So thanks for the heads-up!

Today's Topic: Healing Hurts

Last week I received a letter from a subscriber that was not the first of its kind, but it was serious enough that I thought we could address it together. The few that I've been sent were all from men asking how to approach a new girlfriend after finding out that she was seriously abused in the past. I'm sure there are men out there who have also been abused, but none of them have written to me. Perhaps you'll agree that it merits a discussion.

Generally I like to keep this column light and slightly cheeky, but to be realistic we have to cover the fun side and the darker side of human sexuality. Most of us equate sexuality with pleasure and emotional fulfillment, but for every high there is an opposite and equal low, especially when someone has been abused.

It's in the news so often that we turn a blind eye to human suffering and sexual abuse. High schools discuss it, writers churn out screenplays about it, and musicians write songs about it. But when it happens to you or someone you love, there's no amount of preparation in the world that will make it acceptable.

The letters from my readers varied from frustration to anger, but they all shared a bottom line concern which was "How can I help her get through this, and when will we be able to establish a healthy sexual relationship?" Let me remind you that I am not a doctor, so the best I can offer is a supportive shoulder or some constructive parallel stories that will let you know that you are not at all alone.

Sexual abuse has no pattern. It can be verbal, physical, or emotional, but it all leaves trauma in its path. I'm not the first to remind you that sexual abuse very rarely has anything to do with sex. The abuser is often expressing anger or rage. I've read several articles that hypothesize this behavior as a need to control or dominate. Most people who have suffered through this will recall a feeling of powerlessness or feeling totally helpless. While many think that the physical act is what leaves the damage behind, most victims will tell you that it was like having their soul stolen away. They're left with emotional damage that cannot be verbalized. A once-confident person can be completely changed by the experience while another might be able to work through it short term.

I don't know you or your partners and couldn't begin to understand the nuances of your relationship, but I keep getting the same question, "How do I make this go away?" Again, there is no cure or panacea I can offer. I would highly recommend couples counseling so you can both verbalize your frustrations. Speaking with a professional will not only open a dialogue to promote healing, but they will often give you exercises or strategies to help you get through the tougher parts. This way you can begin to heal together.

The frustration is easy to understand. You both love each other, you want the relationship, she doesn't hold you responsible for what happened (in many cases the abuse happened prior to your meeting), yet you can't seem to make it any better.

The first thing you must exercise is patience. It's not up to you or her. She has no more control over her feelings than you do, so you can't treat it like something that needs to be fixed. She feels your frustration, so the situation becomes more inflamed because she now feels guilty about the fact that she's unable to perform sexually. It's not an easy cycle to break, so the first step is to establish a platform. See if you can both agree that there is a problem. If one partner feels there is a problem and the other doesn't, you can't initiate a change. The decision to seek help must be unanimous, or it won't happen.

The second thing you have to remember is not to push her in any direction. When I say "push," I don't mean pressure to have sex. It could be as simple as letting her discuss her feelings when she's ready and not before. Abuse is devastating, and it has no time limit. If you're the type of person who bounces back from adversity, don't expect her to have your resilience. Most people have trouble understanding why other people don't handle things like they do, and that can lead to more problems. She isn't you. She isn't going to handle this situation like you, so be understanding.

The third and final suggestion I have is for both of you to be prepared for anything. After seeking counsel you might find that she shouldn't be involved with anyone at this point. You might also find that she requires more of your time and attention. I can only imagine how many ways it could turn out, but I am certain that you need to do this together. Healing any relationship involves both parties, so depending on how serious your relationship is, make an educated decision. My heart goes out to any person who has suffered abuse, but remember that we're on this planet together so no one should have to go through this alone. I welcome any support from my readers about this and will most certainly print any letters that can shed light on this subject. Thank you for writing about something so personal. I take great pride in the fact that you find my attention worthy.

♡ ♡ ♡ ♡ ♡ Reader Comments ♡ ♡ ♡ ♡ ♡

Dear Carmen,

I wanted to ask if you have any advice for a lady who has been abused by several men, sexually, mentally and physically. How can she give love to her man when she has so many memories of bad things? Do you know what would cause a man to get angry if his partner was unable to have sexual intercourse due to her memories of the past? Does that mean there is something wrong with him because he gets angry with her for not having intercourse? Thanks so much for your time.

[It's not anger; it's frustration. Every man wants to feel that he should be treated with a clean slate, but punishing the sons for the sins of the father is an unfortunate side effect of abuse. You should both seek guidance from a qualified professional to get through this together.]

Dear Carmen,

My name is X, and I am an Israeli 26-year-old girl. When I read your article "Healing Hurts," I felt that I had to write you about my experience. Almost two years ago I was sexually assaulted. Luckily it was only an assault, and I wasn't raped. But I think that the result is the same. For more than a year I didn't do anything about it until I started to have nightmares and anxiety attacks. It was then when I met my boyfriend who is the most wonderful person I ever met. He was so patient! The first three months were really difficult. Every time we started sex the flashbacks came too, and I would start shaking and crying. Every time it happened he stopped the intercourse and gave me a big hug and reassured me that as long as he is with me, nobody will touch me against my will again.

Hearing that helped me. Besides that, I started seeing a social worker for treatment sessions, and my boyfriend was the most supportive among the people I know. We have an agreement that every time I go to treatment, I call and tell him what happened during the session. Actually he even suggested to go there with me few times in order to learn how to help me. What I'm trying to say is that those men who are asking how to help their new girlfriend get over a sexual assault or rape should, sometimes, learn to just listen to the woman's needs. One woman will need to talk about it over and over, and another one will want to stay quiet or just ignore what happened to her. But whatever she decides, you should support her. That's at least what helped me go through the worst part of the healing. I hope that by bringing my experience to this column I'll be able to help other people who are in the same situation I was few months ago.

Dear Carmen,

First, let me say how much I enjoy your mailings. I truly appreciate all of your columns. I am ready to turn 35 this year and am just now coming out of my sexual shell due, in large degree, to sexual abuse starting at the age of three. It no longer bothers me to talk about it. What bothers me is that we've started into the 21st century with gigantic leaps in science and technology and yet, as a culture, we've no more clue how to deal with this atrocity than we did two hundred years ago when no one spoke of it. You're right; there is no "quick fix." This is due, I believe, to the fact that sexual abuse leaves behind such a multi-faceted wound spiritually, emotionally, and physically.

I am in no way a professional in the field of healing lives, but I do have a pretty extensive personal background in psychiatry (no small surprise) and a degree in pre-med. I'd be happy to correspond with anyone who thinks it would be beneficial, male or female, abused or the supporter. Thinking that I might help someone to take a first deep breath without the weight of guilt choking them or just bring a smile to someone who hasn't had one in too long would be an honor. I don't know how that works on your list, but you may post my e-mail address, my letter or mention that someone is willing to correspond. Whatever is fine. But I'd like to help if I can. Thanks for reading this, and again, for a wonderful column. It's people like you with straight-forward, nonthreatening dialog like this that can reopen a world for people who've lived with the door shut far too long.

♡ ♡ ♡ ♡ ♡ ♡ ♡ ♡ ♡ ♡ ♡ ♡ ♡ ♡ ♡ ♡ ♡ ♡

Today's Topic: Sexually Challenged, My Ass!

While writing about many sensitive subjects, I've become quite used to writing about the topics that nobody really wants to tackle. No problem. I'm not here to win a popularity contest, but what I have noticed is a lack of information or even interest about sexual endeavors concerning the disabled. I got a letter a while back from a man in a wheelchair stating that most people don't even consider this an issue because disabled individuals are not looked upon as sexual beings. Nothing could be further from the truth, and it's only fitting that we discuss this, too! I don't know who that man was, but I thank him for his letter.

Sorry about the blunt heading, but the last time anyone actually addressed this was in the movie *The Deer Hunter* or the occasional after school special. The thing to remember is that for every person with a crutch or a wheelchair, there is a different reason for every situation. It might be ALS, MS, osteoporosis, spinal injury, or PMS that you see. So whatever you do, don't assume anything!

The fact that someone would be dismissed as a sexual candidate based on their situation is poor judgment. Try talking to them first before you decide. Chances are you might find them disagreeable for reasons other than the impairment! These people have an equal chance at being charming, passionate, sensual, or dull as dirt! You see where this is going, right? The only barrier lies in the eyes of the beholder, so let's just move on.

One of the biggest mistakes you can make when dealing with someone with a disability is to assume that they don't feel things like you do. Emotionally that's wrong, but physically it's also wrong. People with nerve damage can be motor impaired without being sensitivity impaired or the other way around, but it doesn't mean that they don't have the same desires. If you get to know someone well enough (disabled or not), they'll let you know how to handle the physical aspect of the relationship. So far the rules sound pretty similar, right?

A woman wrote about how her husband was paralyzed in a car accident and ever since, their sex life was better than ever. I've also had people tell me that after something physically traumatic happened, their sex life was over. These stories were as unique as the people themselves, so making a blanket statement would be wrong. I guess what makes it sad is when you find out that people equate their sexuality with just one small body part. For 95 issues of "Great Sexpectations" I've tried to bring home the point that great sex begins in the mind and should be a total body experience. Physical attraction, arousal, and intercourse is not limited to the perfectly able-bodied, and many people could be dismissing something really great by making snap judgments.

I watched a soap the other day with this total hunk of an actor who plays a disabled doctor. What can I say but hubba hubba! I'm 99% positive that he is truly disabled, and I would honestly get in line for his company. It was refreshing to see this, but by the same token, he represented that standard of soap opera beauty that most of us can only dream about. I give credit to ABC for bringing him to the show, and they didn't cut him any slack in the gorgeous department, either. If all the other actors have to be model perfect, so did he! They also went out on a limb by throwing him into a few bedroom scenes (yes, I watched), and what amazed me was how natural the whole thing was.

I'm not suggesting that there are no changes in the routines. It might be as simple as a location preference or the introduction of a few extra pillows, but the point is to define an experience just like you would with anyone else. If there are physical adaptations, those too can be easily accommodated. The greatest error you can make is a misguided assumption. I really need to hear from my readers out there, and to find out if any of you know who that actor is (nudge, wink, smile)!

♡ ♡ ♡ ♡ ♡ Ɍeader Comments ♡ ♡ ♡ ♡ ♡

Dear Carmen,

I want to thank you for this column. I was disabled in a car accident 25 years ago. The total sex rehab I got was, and I quote, "You can still have children." On the other hand, a man that had about the same level injury that I did, had special therapy three times a week. Oh well, I have heard that things have finally changed about that. But I spent the first 21 years trying to figure out if I was sexually attractive to anyone. I am still working around a number of different things, but I finally know that being sexually attractive to the opposite sex is not based on my disability. If he feels that way then he is shallow, and I really don't want him in my life anyway. Thank you for your time.

Hey Carmen,

I love your column. I just wanted to comment on the disabled issue. My mom has cerebral palsy. She has been married four times and has three children and two grandchildren. Kids love riding and climbing on her scooter. When I was 13, a friend had me ask my mom how she had sex. My mom's answer was, "I am handicapped, not dead!"

Hi, Carmen,

My man uses a walker due to a genetic disability, but I assure you that he is very able in the bed or wherever we choose to make love. There is no lack of desire and a very limited lack of ability. He is the sexiest, most sensual man I have known. "Able-bodied" men have not been able to move me and bring me to heights the way that he does. Do not count anyone out because they may have a physical disability!

From a devoted reader

Today's Topic: Personality or IQ?

Just like everyone else, I find myself constantly amazed by human nature. When you think you have a pretty fair measure of what makes people tick, you'll see something that just flies in the face of logic. I've never claimed to have all of the answers, but this time I'll invite my readers to chime in with some reflections.

I've seen hundreds of couples that amaze me. We've all been there. You're at a restaurant or bar where you see what you think is the most mismatched couple of all time. Sometimes one is obviously brighter than the other, or one exudes charm and wit while the other watches the paint dry, or one is just out of diapers while the other is ready for Social Security. No matter how opposite they look, I'm not judging-- I'm just observing. Who am I to say what one person is attracted to? Hey, if it works for you, go for it! I guess my confusion revolves around the physical versus. the intellectual. It's the last showdown at the cerebral corral, and I need some help.

Recently, I've had the pleasure of meeting some up-market executive types for another company I work with. Granted they were all men, but what I knew about these high rollers were their attributes. These guys are all sophisticated, attractive, worldly, brilliant, wealthy, and so on. Maybe I watch too many old movies, but I was expecting to find a reasonable compliment to their personalities when I met their (very lucky) wives. I'm not so cliche that I thought they were married to women who matched them on all levels, but I assumed that they matched in a few aspects, right? Wrong.

I was amazed to see that one was involved with a very loud/animated partner, while the other was attached to a simple creature with a penchant for shopping. I was amazed! What about finding a partner who can stimulate you physically, as well as intellectually? What about matching wits and speaking a subtle language that only you two understand? Apparently I've been misled. With men receiving so much negative press about commitment fears or running from code-pendent women, I thought the times were-a-changin.' Aren't men looking for a certain independence or a smattering of intellectual wit? Does it always boil down to physical traits or chemical attraction? I'm lost. Are men secretly more attracted to the simple types who need help balancing the checkbook? Do they relish the midmorning call reminding her to turn off the coffee pot or not run the car when the garage door is closed?

Movies haven't helped this quandary either. The great guy always ends up with the great gal, and they've saturated us with movies about men who freak-out when faced with being...dare I say it...needed! Clark Gable didn't want the southern waif mealy-mouthed little milksop in *Gone With The Wind*. He wanted that in-your-face no mincing words Scarlett O'Hara! I smell a rat. What I'm being taught is not being sup-ported in reality. Can I just say with pride that I've never once disinte-grated into a little pouting ball of anger because I wanted my guy to buy me something shiny. As a matter of fact, I'm very clumsy about accepting any gifts, let alone expecting one from a partner.

So why am I amazed? Because the men I'm surrounded by are all involved with those high-maintenance pouty little "Bring me to Tiffany's" crew. I'm astounded. What am I missing? What woman in her right mind would adopt such a 1940's cliche persona and expect it to work? More importantly, why are these guys married to them?

Help me out here. We need to talk. I feel that physical attraction is the touchstone for most relationships, but if you don't click mentally it's all over. Right? How many of you have been fixed up with some mouth-watering paragon of sexual prowess, but the minute the conversation started, you wanted to run screaming for the door? If you're going to tell me that sometimes one of the partners needs to feel more superior, I can accept that, but does it really go that far? Are there hoards of women married to men without any perceptible intelligence, too?

As you can see, this is one of those forums that needs further discussion. Am I missing something totally obvious? I always followed the phrase "water seeks its own level," but this time I'm drowning. Write to me and see if we can get a feel for what's really going on out there. Please don't write to me about Anna Nicole Smith, either. I'm talking about something less blatant here. Notice I didn't say these women were Playboy centerfolds? That's not the case. My confusion surrounds this whole dichotomy. Carmen needs help. Write about your observations so I can tell if I'm on target or just losing my little mind!

Wow! My inquiry about dynamic men who marry women who seem so completely opposite got quite a wave of responses. The common denominator offered in most of the letters revolved around the need to feel superior or needed. Of course I realize that things are not always as they seem on the surface, but I wasn't talking about older executives who married their high school/college sweethearts, either. I was talking about younger men who choose curious matches, and the following is just a sample of responses:

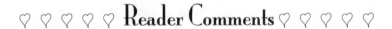

♡ ♡ ♡ ♡ ♡ **Reader Comments** ♡ ♡ ♡ ♡ ♡

Dear Carmen,

Quite frankly, I believe men want dependent women. Most men anyway. I was married for nearly 17 years. At the beginning we were both working full-time jobs. Basically, I took care of the house, and he took care of the cars. He joined the Army. Over the years, he was gone, and I became more independent out of necessity. This did not go over very well. Eventually, he decided I wanted to run things. He wanted what I call the "Donna Reed" wife with a pretty little apron and not much initiative. I just wanted to share my opinion with you. Thanks for letting me blow off some steam.

Dear Carmen,

Your mistake is thinking that those men were intelligent. I have found that most "successful," wealthy men are not very intelligent. They tend to be salesmen at heart. They may be extremely personable, may have one area of expertise and are almost universally manipulative. However, they tend to be shallow with an unwarranted (but only superficial) confidence in their own intellect. If this is challenged, it can cost them their self-esteem. Is it any wonder that they tend to end up with women who cannot challenge that? Intelligent women can be hard to find as well. Many intelligent women have a habit of hiding their brains, believing that all men are afraid of them and that they are better off just being a pretty face. Ain't life a bitch?

Dear Carmen;

I just read about what men are attracted to, and I can tell you that I personally like a woman that stimulates my mind as well as my body. There has to be a certain amount of looks, but If it isn't there when they open their mouth, then I'm not interested. But getting back to your question. Maybe some of these men are so used to being in power that they don't want someone of equal power but someone of lesser smarts that treat them like they are gods.

[Suddenly I'm imagining an altar and small animal sacrifice.]

Dear Carmen,

Firstly, I think that both you and your newsletter are great! As for today's issue, I just wanted to add my little bit. Usually I think you are pretty spot-on with your sketches about people and their behaviors, though I feel today you missed the mark. Something I have observed (in my own relationships and with other couples) is a distinct difference between public and private. This means that people can and often do choose to show just certain aspects of themselves in public, while letting their true selves unravel in the comfort (not just physically speaking here) and intimacy of their relationship. If the old maxim "don't judge a book by its cover" is applied here, we certainly should be cautious about judging a relationship by what those in it care to let us glimpse. In other words, you have no idea what those women are really like, do you? Anyway, keep informing and impressing us as you have so graciously done for as long as you feel the inclination to do so! Happy New Year!

[Well noted. Cheers, mate!]

Hi Carmen!

Let me boost your ego and tell you the wife and I REALLY enjoy your column. Now to the matter at hand. I always ask people, "Do you know why you are living here?" They always answer, "No, why am I living here?" I reply, "because your ancestors, the "settlers," stopped their oxen and wagon here and built a home. Why do you think they called them settlers? They totally settled to live here, and I believe we haven't learned from our ancestors' mistakes. We as human beings want and need to be appreciated and cherished. Unfortunately we mistake this feeling for love instead of friendship. People that are what we called "mismatched" have fallen into this. Or how about people that are codependant? A lot of people out there are co-dependant. To me, being co-dependant is a leftover trait of our ancestors. It's called being too lazy to go and find exactly what makes you happy. All I can say is don't settle.....you DON'T HAVE TO! Keep up the non-biased opinions! Lord knows I can't!

♡ ♡ ♡ ♡ ♡ ♡ ♡ ♡ ♡ ♡ ♡ ♡ ♡ ♡ ♡ ♡ ♡ ♡ ♡ ♡

Today's Topic: Nice Guy Curse

You've read the letters in reader comments, you've questioned it yourself, and chances are you're no closer to an answer about the dreaded Nice Guy Syndrome. Does this curse really exist? What woman in her right mind would break up with a sweet, sensitive, and caring man to take up with a man who appears to be indifferent or ill-mannered? Are they really treating their women too nicely, or is it something else?

Perhaps you remember the letter I printed in reader comments a few weeks ago. Some poor tortured soul wrote in about the fact that the woman he treated like gold broke up with him to take up with someone he considered several links down on the food chain. After scrutinizing his relationship, he sarcastically declared to attract his next mate by losing his job, using foul language, and practicing less than a sound hygiene regiment. I wouldn't want to discourage anyone from trying to improve their romantic endeavors, but I think there's a better way to handle this situation.

What's really happening here has nothing to do with being too nice. Women have no problems with nice; they have a problem with ambivalence, passivity, androgynous behavior, and a wishy-washy demeanor. Women are attracted to confidence and strength, but when there's no conflict (yes dear, no dear), it leads to boredom and hostility.

You know you've entered the first stages of "nice guydom" when you notice your gal becoming slightly more acidic with you. Her attitude will cool, and you'll notice that she no longer asks you for your opinion because you've lost yourself.

Rule number one is never lose yourself to a woman. You can't wrap your whole world around her without sacrificing your individuality. Most women adore a man who has a sense of himself and knows who he is. It goes beyond just knowing who you are; it entails asserting yourself and honoring your ideals. Don't change them to agree with her. If you do, she'll see how much of a doormat you can be. I'm not saying that women take a cruel interest in pushing someone a little too hard. It has more to do with pushing for a reaction. Any reaction would be welcome except another "okay, whatever you say." Disintegrating into a spineless wonder only creates more hostility.

Pretty soon she'll be pushing the envelope just to see if there's anyone home! It sounds childish, but it's not. If you can't fight for yourself, she's going to think you can't fight for her, either. It lies deep in the DNA to want to feel protected. Notice the word protected as opposed to bullied. A woman doesn't want to be told what to do. She wants to be respected. Sometimes the nice guy syndrome leads to lack of self-respect. No woman respects a man who doesn't respect himself first. I'm certain it works the other way around as well.

What's the solution? It's more like a few strategies to keep from falling into this pattern. It works best if you challenge your woman from time to time by not giving in. Yes, it's polite to ask what she would prefer, but assert your own preferences rather than always caving into her will. It's not rude; it's just part of keeping the relationship honest. I'm certain that there were a few guys out there that didn't want to see *Titanic* right? That's all I'm saying. There should be equal give and take over decisions no matter if it's dinner choices or who gets on top!

Passivity is the number one killer of relationships. Not only should you act on what you say, you need to act in ways that entail more than just the remote. Sometimes it's the sedentary that suffer more break-ups. Surprise her with your capacity to be spontaneous, and part of that means not asking her permission to be spontaneous! That would just put you back to square one in the jellyfish game.

Just to recap, it's not the nice guys that are being dumped. It's the killer trio of passivity, boredom, and lack of self-confidence that will effectively end all romance. Passion thrives on pushing buttons. If you remove your buttons, she'll have nothing to push!

I can not wait to get this batch of mail! Please let me know if you agree or not. Also, clue me in on your experiences, if any, with this syndrome so we can have fun in a few Fridays during reader comments. I'm not asking your permission to end this. I'm just leaving you! (Deal with it baby!)

♡ ♡ ♡ ♡ ♡ Reader Comments ♡ ♡ ♡ ♡ ♡

Dear Carmen,

I was just curious if girls ever get to a point where there is not a need for head games. Do they grow out of it? I'm not really "looking," but I do feel that I have a lot to offer a girl, and I always seem to make this certain impression just because I was raised with some manners and are polite to people. It would just be refreshing to come across someone who I could speak to like a person without making the "nice guy" impression or heading straight to the friend zone. I have studied this in depth and experimented plenty, and it seems that with most girls, all you have to do is chain them to the stove and call them a bitch, then quit your job to be poor, and they'll love you forever.

I just don't get it. Can you do a little something on this "friend zone" or "you're like a brother to me" thing? I understand that girls like/need a challenge and all that, so here's a challenge: help me not adopt the chauvinistic attitude that all girls are the same with the exception of their cup size. Please prove me wrong. Thanks for your time.

[Okay, my dedicated readers, start writing so we can address this man and his "Friend Zone" question!]

Hi, Carmen:

Great job with the column! I'd like to respond to the man who wrote about the "Friend Zone" question because it's a topic I feel very strongly about. My last boyfriend says the exact same things, that women only look for jerks or players. That's not true. Perhaps I'm an exception among females, but the guys I am most attracted to are the "nice guys," the ones who I know are going to be loyal to me and not be sleeping around, and the ones who take the time to listen to me and love me for reasons other than my cup size (because if we were going by that alone I wouldn't get much loving,' I'll tell you that!).

A word to all the "nice guys" out there--trust me, a lot of women seem to only want the show-offs and players, but in reality once they get hurt enough and are through with casual relationships, they don't mean anything. They'll come to you when they're ready for the serious relationships. In the meantime, rest assured that the world needs more guys like you, so don't trade in your manners and sweetness for arrogance and casual flings. You're worth far more than that. Take care.

Dear Carmen,

To the reader who wants to get out of the "Friend Zone" without turning into a pig: watch the movie *You've Got Mail* with Tom Hanks and Meg Ryan. Pay attention, but ignore the part with the coffee shop. Give it a little bit of time and instead of shopping for books together, she'll take you to Victoria's Secret. Instead of going out for a drink together, you'll stay in for dinner and wine. When the time is right, she'll ask YOU if you want to take things further. The danger: don't let it get to the point that you're another one of her "girlfriends," someone that she sees as a very good, completely platonic friend. Another useful tip--if you're really a good catch but she doesn't see it, meet her friends and let *them* tell her how wonderful you are, rather than trying to impress her yourself (which almost ALWAYS fails, unless you fail so miserably that it's "cute"). This works best with friends that aren't single (who might want you, or be jealous that you want her and not them), but who also don't have "alpha-male wanna-be" boyfriends who will go out of their way to make you look "wussy."

Carmen,

In response to the women who desire bad boys or jerks:

To date I have had some of the same experiences as this reader. Women seem to dump me for losers. I keep falling for someone from whom I can't win approval and basically get downright emotional abuse. Ask your readers to take a test: write a list of the names of all previous emotionally-attached romantic partners, whether it's been sexual or not. Now, under each one, write down all the negative aspects of that person or relationship (only the negative). Circle all the traits or negative things that match. All the same, right? On another paper write all the negative emotions associated with "home" or childhood at the parent's.

Guess what? For most people in my and your other reader's situation, the "home"-related negative emotional feelings or traits match the negative ones we've encountered thus far in partners! The point? Learn to stop going after Mom or Dad. Recognize when one is attracted to past emotional intensity.

[Thank you for the very appropriate test.]

Hi, Carmen,

I just finished reading the reader comments. I'd just like to tell all of those nice single guys out there not to give up! You'll find that special someone. Do not change your standards because women that are worth being with do not want the jerks and players. They want the honest down to earth guy. Someone made a comment that women are only attracted to the jerks and players. Well my problem is all I seem to *find* are jerks and players. Where are all of these nice honest guys? That's what I would like to know!

[They're out there! Trust me...]

Carmen:

I just wanted to say your advice on the "nice guy syndrome" was right on time; I couldn't have said it better myself. I hope all the nice guys out there will take your advice given on this topic and even the not-so-nice guys can learn from this. Keep up the good work.

Dear Carmen,

Okay so nice guys don't get dumped for being nice, but for being wishy- washy and passive. So is that the same reason men are attracted to bitchy women? 90% of the men I've run across are just totally drawn to truly bitchy women. It seems like the worse these women treat them, the better they like it. They'll even dump a nice girl to be with a woman that treats them like shit. What is with these guys?

Dear Carmen,

I usually read these messages and take something away with me, but today really ruffled my feathers! About your advice on men not losing themselves to a woman--why not? When two people find many things in common, they enjoy each other's company, their sexual compatibility is wonderful, so why not give into each other? This article comes off as a man being an asshole again! They don't need that! They are labeled unfeeling, selfish, stupid, egotistical, you name it. Why can't a man be heartfelt and weigh the feelings and/or situation and still come out being a sweetie! This one is for the garbage can, Carmen!

♡ ♡ ♡ ♡ ♡ ♡ ♡ ♡ ♡ ♡ ♡ ♡ ♡ ♡ ♡ ♡ ♡ ♡ ♡ ♡

Today's Topic: Teen Concerns

In response to the deluge of mail you've sent, I've decided to address some of the topics that require more than a one-sentence explanation. In particular, I've been asked by some of my younger readers to discuss issues about pregnancy, virginity, multiple partners, and peer pressure. I hope this clarifies some of the misinformation and confusion.

I'll begin with one of the most important concerns I have with younger couples who practice "pulling out" before a full ejaculation. This does NOT prevent pregnancy! There are sperm present in the smallest drop of seminal fluid, so please realize that when a man gets wet and ready to have intercourse, sperm is already present. Please know that pulling out is not a prevention against pregnancy.

For those of you who take birth control pills, you already know that it's about 99% effective until you take antibiotics. For anything from a sinus infection to postoperative treatment, doctors prescribe antibiotics for a myriad of reasons. These antibiotics interfere with your birth control pills which most women don't know. Drug companies have only recently included warning labels on drugs like Cipro and Floxin explaining that they render most hormones useless. If you find yourself taking antibiotics for any reason, PLEASE use an additional form of birth control.

I've also received many letters from younger couples about how to approach the question of sex if one of the partners is a virgin. I have no easy answer for this because the reasons for intimacy are as individual as snowflake patterns. No two are the same. What I can say is that true intimacy starts in the heart, and some of the most meaningful relationships do not involve sex. If the question becomes inevitable, discuss your needs at length and then prepare yourself for any changes you're going to make. I had one letter from a man who is 23 whose girlfriend is 17 asking how to approach the subject. Try an appropriate time without making it feel like a pressure situation and see what she says.

One of my favorite letters covered a very popular sentiment: "Carmen, how do I ask my partner to try new positions or techniques without hurting any feelings?" This should be easy because it doesn't mean that the sex wasn't satisfactory before, you just want to keep things creative. If you want to use a metaphor, try a food comparison. Maybe you love pasta and could eat it everyday, right? Well, sometimes you get a craving for pizza instead, so you order one. That doesn't mean that you still don't love pasta, right? I think you see where this is going. If you use common sense and communicate in a sensitive manner, you'll never go wrong. Someone shared some sage wisdom with me recently in a letter that stated: "There are no great lovers, only great couples!" On that note, I'll return to your letters and dig up some more topics to cover. Remember what Frost said about the path less traveled. Keep writing!

♡ ♡ ♡ ♡ ♡ Reader Comments ♡ ♡ ♡ ♡ ♡

Dear Carmen,

I met a boy, who at the time was 19 and a virgin, which I thought was great. I never had anyone to teach me about sex and to let me know that it was something special! I know I should have already known that but how, when no one talked to me about it? Well, I was not a virgin, obviously. It's been three years and now he tries to make me feel bad for mistakes I have made in the past and for my doings! I already hate myself enough for just not knowing. I am so in love and I am now scared he is either tryng to venture out or has and is trying to blame me! I know you are busy and don't answer really, but if anyone else is having a problem like this, could you give me a little advice?!

[Anyone trying to berate you for past mistakes is not a caring partner. Stop beating yourself up and consider your history a learning experience designed to empower your future decisions. If he really wants to go, he'll find any excuse no matter how flimsy.]

Carmen~

Your last newsletter really spoke to me! I am a 16-year-old female, and I was thinking about letting my boyfriend pressure me into sex. After reading your letter and feeling that protectiveness in the end, I was totally turned around! Thank you for caring about us young teenagers. I sent my boyfriend packing and feel much better about myself!

Today's Topic: More Teen Concerns

After sorting through hundreds of emails, it has become painfully clear that many of you are far under the age of 18. While this column was not meant for young teens, some of you have put me in a position to answer some questions that have me greatly concerned. Perhaps we should cover some of the most basic, yet popular concerns.

I am in no way promoting or advocating young teen sex. To be precise, anyone who is not beyond the age of 18 should still be listening to The Backstreet Boys and attending slumber parties! However, here in the real world some of you have questioned your newly-discovered sexual feelings, which is, of course, normal. What worries me are the amount of young readers who think that oral sex, anal sex, and reaching orgasm with a hands-only approach is not considered sex. Wrong! As soon as you've ventured near anyone's genitals and performed any kind of fondling to the point of moisture, you're having sex my young friends. I know people who kiss with enough intensity that it's technically sex, so let's try to draw some lines, shall we?

I also have something to say to many of my younger females readers. Boys are always going to be more aggressive about pursuing anything that closely resembles sex. One of my male friends recalled what puberty was like, and in the most accurately humorous comment he remarked, "God! At 13 forget about sex; I was just looking for things it would fit inside of!" Trust me, you don't want to be considered one of those objects a boy just wants to "fit inside of," do you? Any boy that has the misfortune of pressuring you into sex should be sent packing, understand? He's not in love, he's in the same camp as your grandmother's dog who humps anything that accidentally crosses his path.

Now about the letter I got from one girl who reported having 22 sexual partners by the time she was seventeen. The question was, "Carmen, is that too many?" My answer is yes, of course. Technically you can't lock up the barn door after the horse ran away, but you can train the beast when it comes home. You need to experience celibacy and define who you really are as a person. Yes, sex feels good, but it's supposed to be treated as something sacred between two fully-formed adults. It's not bowling; it's intimacy and I have never met a 17-year-old girl who was a fully-realized adult. Nor have I ever met a 17-year-old boy who was, either. I don't care if he does shave every other day.

Some of you have expressed concerns about bleeding with finger penetration, odd scars, pregnancy scares, and other goodies. If you have any question about anything physical, consult a Doctor! I am not an MD, and if something feels wrong, trust your instincts and get yourself checked out, please! Again, I reiterate that most of you under 18 are too young to have sexual relations, and sex involves more than traditional intercourse unlike what you've been told by President Clinton. I'm through ranting now. I care about you all and don't want to see any of you get hurt, so please think before you make another move!

♡ ♡ ♡ ♡ ♡ Reader Comments ♡ ♡ ♡ ♡ ♡

Dear Carmen,

I've only been a short time reader, but I have to say that I'm impressed with what I've heard. I just read your Issue "More Teen Concerns." Being a 19-year-old male, I must say that I agree with everything you're saying. It's always good to hear someone that says it's fine not to rush into things. When I was a little younger, it would have been a comfort to have someone sit down with me and be as open as you've been in your discussions. I must admit that at 19, I still don't know everything there is to know and still sometimes stop and wonder what exactly is going on. I personally have only been with two people sexually and been "all the way" with one. Unfortunately, she was raped earlier this year by a 42-year-old man. It's a bit uncomfortable to think of a 17-year-old carrying a 42-year-old's baby, but I'm sorry to say that's exactly how it ended up. I don't want to get off on my own rant, so I'll be off for now. Keep up the good work.

[It sounds like you're treating her with understanding and concern. I hope everything turns out well for you both.]

Dear Carmen,

My name is X. I just turned 16 July 6th of 2000, and I have a daughter who is almost 13 months old. I totally agree with everything you have to say in your "Great Sexpectations" e-mails. I understand that having sex at a young age is wrong and that we teens haven't matured enough to completely give ourselves to a man/woman. But some of us have been forced to grow up and we think that we are old enough to handle things like that. I, for instance, thought I was old enough to have sex with a guy that I thought loved me, but it turned out that all he wanted was sex from me. Now that I am a single teen mother with his child, he doesn't help out with money or spend a lot of time with his daughter, but I do believe that I have matured and learned from my pregnancy and my life. There are a few teens out there (under the age of 18) that know life and are old enough at heart to handle the pressures of sex. Thanks.

[I received several letters just like this one.]

Carmen,

I have trouble meeting and asking woman out. I am either too shy or am not sure if they are interested or not. I am 18 years old and looking for some help, so I bow before your wisdom.

[If you're not sure, try some subtle flirtation and see if she reacts positively. If she returns the flirting, you've got a green light.]

Today's Topic: Green-Eyed Monsters

Logically we all know in our hearts that jealousy is not only destructive behavior, but it undermines the integrity of any relationship. Oddly enough we may have the intelligence to know better, but sometimes it's like the car wreck you can't turn away from. Perhaps we should address the darker side of romance yet again.

I watched it happen last night. One happy couple enters the room for an evening of polite conversation and socializing with friends. As the evening progressed and more joined the little gathering, I noticed that one half of the happy couple (the gal) changed her body language.

At first it looked subtle. She turned her chair around so she could watch everyone, and I do mean everyone. She was still chatting pleasantly to everyone, but while she was talking with one person she was looking only at her boyfriend and observing who he was talking to.

Well, it's obvious when someone is talking to you but looking away from you, that they're not terribly engaged. Because she was so intensely focused on her boyfriend, I found myself really watching their interactions for the rest of the night.

Nothing too drastic happened, but by the end of the evening she was lighting his cigarettes (she doesn't smoke) and shadowing his moves. You know what I mean, right? She would hand him his drink and then set it down, hold his jacket, and feed him gum when she thought he wanted some. There wasn't any real communication, just physical insistence. The dead giveaway was when she stopped talking completely to take care of his every whim. Finally, by the end of the night she started muttering about how one group of girls was looking at him with too much interest, and he's too cute to just leave alone, and how she was ready to snap into action if one more girl checked him out in an obvious way.

Wow. You know this pattern all too well, and while nothing major happened, what I witnessed screamed volumes. He did nothing wrong. There was no gratuitous flirting or cause for concern, yet she was pacing around him like she was on duty. Why? Jealousy is not rational, and it doesn't follow the rules of logic. There are situations that might draw this out, but when there's no discernible conflict you have to ask yourself a few key questions.

First of all identify the reasons for your jealous feelings:

1. Do you have a history of dating men/women who have cheated on you? If you have had this experience more than once, you need to find out why you are drawn to people who are less than monogamous. Perhaps you attract this because you don't really desire monogamy yourself or you're always looking for the fatal flaw that will keep you from trusting anyone ever again. Most people in this predicament

have been hurt very deeply in the past, and they have not been able to trust or move on since. By acting in a jealous manner they are perhaps sending signals to their partner that this isn't going to last, so if they're going to hurt you, they better do it now before you're in this relationship up to your eyeballs.

2. What originally attracted you to your current partner? If you were smitten by flirtation or overwhelmed by his/her confidence and charm, you're not alone. Oddly enough, the thing you were most attracted to can also become the trait that tears you apart. It was okay to be confident and charming at first, but inside you wish that others didn't see the same thing you did. You went from coveting these qualities to resenting them all in a short time span. Try not to punish the sons for the sins of the father. I know you've lived through this too many times, but try to approach each relationship with a clean slate, "tabula rasa." This is not always easy, but it's worth trying if you want to break the pattern.

3. Have you personally cheated on anyone that you were involved with, even if it was only once? This one is all about the ghost of guilty behavior. Even though you would never ever do it again in a million years and swore on a stack of bibles, there's a little voice in your head that says, "Well, if even I'm capable of such unsavory behavior, then surely anyone I date in the future could certainly do the same thing!" You can see where this is going. Most jealous behavior is rooted in abject insecurity or lack of confidence. The person you're with might be clueless that you're harboring such feelings, so try to get it out in the open.

The real shame of jealous behavior is that it destroys relationships that might otherwise have a chance at smooth sailing. Nine times out of ten it works as a self-fulfilling prophecy. If you think it enough, you might just will it to happen. If your partner knows you suffer through this madness, they'll probably tire of always being on the defensive and just give up. What's the use of staying with someone who has no trust? It's more than jealousy, it's the question of why? What did you do to make this person jealous? Probably nothing. They just have their own little internal drama, and unfortunately you have no control over it.

I know that some people think a little jealousy is healthy. The occasional display of territorial pissing makes us feel special, right? That may be so, but make sure its not a regular display. Exercise extreme moderation when it comes to acting jealous. It can be easily misunderstood, and it might cause more harm in the end. Yes, I'm only human and I would like to think that my man would rush to defend my honor if some stranger started mauling me in public, but that situation doesn't present itself every day--at least not in my world!

♡ ♡ ♡ ♡ ♡ Reader Comments ♡ ♡ ♡ ♡ ♡

Dear Carmen,

Thank you for your letter. It really helped me see myself. I have just come through a year and a half of being terribly jealous! But, of course, I thought I had reason, and to a certain extent I did. It all started very innocently with an e-mail to a classmate web-site to an old schoolmate! I even encouraged my fiance to write to her! I felt secure in our relationship and didn't worry about this. At first we shared her e-mail to him. He would tell me, "I got a letter today." Pretty soon things escalated to private mail, and I would find out later she wrote. Then the phone calls started, one to two hours long, then two secret trips to Washington state just to visit an old friend. Well, as you can see, I became the sleuthing stalker and insanely jealous. Our relationship began to deteriorate rapidly. The more jealous I became, the more underground he went. To make a long story short, he said this relationship was only on paper (yes, to him, but I'm sure she felt differently!), not to mention cards in the mail, candy by e-mail, and roses! Anyway, I got to the point of "you want this, you can have this." I'm out of here and moved to another state for three months. He came around and cleaned his relationship corner, and now everything is wonderful! But every once in a while some little thing triggers my jealousy, so I have to remember that sometimes, nothing is nothing, sometimes not! Thanks for listening. I really enjoy your newsletter and have definitely learned a lot!

Dear Carmen

Once again this was another great letter. Sad to say it's all too true in my situation. I was with a very nice lady and all seemed well at first. Eventually the green-eyed monster reared its head and never left. She accused me of sleeping around when I go on business trips, and I don't. She says all men that travel sleep around. We didn't function well in mixed groups because she was alway eyeing the opposition. We were great when we were alone. I finally couldn't take it anymore and just faced up to the fact that she had been dumped on before and that had injured her for the rest of all men.

Carmen,

I really appreciated your column on jealousy, and it came at a really good time in my life. My ex-boyfriend and I broke up about two months ago for many many reasons, and I believe that one of them may have been his jealous behavior. He wouldn't let me have a moment alone, constantly wondering where I was and what I was doing, and didn't want me talking to another guy (or girl for that matter) for fear that I would cheat on him. I do not have a history of cheating on people, however he has a heavy history of cheating on his girlfriends with guys and vice versa. I believe that his behavior led him to believe that I would do the same thing, to the point where he doesn't understand that I'm not even interested in girls. He did end up cheating on me, several times I found out, and we broke up about two months ago. I started another relationship with a guy last week, and just last night I noticed someone in the show he's in hitting on him. I couldn't just sit through his rehearsal and watch him to make sure he wouldn't do anything, so I just said goodbye and had to trust him. I found this incredibly difficult to do because of my last relationship. After reading your column and thinking about my last relationship, I realize that I may cause something to happen just by my mistrust. I think it's definitely true that if you think something's going to happen, it will. It's like that for everything. If you think positively, things will occur, whereas if you constantly think the worst, that's what you're going to get, with few exceptions. I just wanted to say thank you for making me think, as you always do.

Carmen,

Thank you for your current issue on jealousy. It really opened my eyes. My boyfriend is always getting tired of me saying, "If one more girl looks at you..." meanwhile he's not doing a thing. He doesn't flirt with them and doesn't initiate it. He doesn't do anything but shower me with love and adoration, and yet everytime I see a pretty girl even glancing around and her glance travels over him, I get mean and nasty and somehow turn it around to blame it on him. I didn't really think much of it, even when he told me he was getting tired of going through this with me because he would never leave me or cheat on me, I still wouldn't let it go. But then in your column you said that eventually the person will just give up trying to explain that they're not going to cheat, and they'll get so tired of being on the defensive that they'll just leave. Wow. That made me think. "Oh my gosh... what if that happens?" etc. etc. Thank you. I will work on my jealousy and hopefully be able to calm down when he talks to a female friend of his who also has a boyfriend. :)

Dear Carmen,

Good reading, Carmen. Unfortunately, I struggle every day with jealousy, and your e-mail will help me deal with it. I will definitely follow your advice. Thanks!

Dear Carmen,

Sad but true. I just broke up with someone (because of my jealous ways) whom I am still deeply in love with. He knows I'm the jealous type, but doesn't know to what extremes my jealousy takes me to. I would get mad at him for just being happy. (Because I'm constantly jealous of anyone or anything that might make him happy other than me.) I'd be mad at him for things only I noticed and he was clueless about. I am now lonely, sad, hurt and I regret every single time I've been mad at him for the wrong reasons (my crazy reasons). I miss him and would love to change my ways, but I think it might be too late for our relationship.

Yes, jealousy is an insecurity. It's a demon!

Carmen,

You hit the nail on the head for me. My current relationship is failing because she has been so jealous. Not always of my friendly flirting, which as you said was charming when she met me, but my friendships with both men and woman. Because I have healthy friendships that are nurturing and close and supportive, and she isn't as open and trusting with her friends, my relationships are cause for many argurments. I am still trying to keep the peace, but as a friend once said "the jar is almost empty." Yes, we have discussed the issue. What she does now is not say anything and just treats me differently, so no help there. Anyway, thanks for letting me know, rightly in my mind, that it's not just me. What a relief.

Hi, Carmen!

You were right when you said that sometimes the one thing that attracts you to someone can tear you apart. I am attracted to suave and charming guys. When we finally have an "agreement," I start getting jealous. I always think that if I found him charming, then there must be other girls who do, too! I'm scared of girls taking him away from me!

One more thing, I am insecure with myself, and I admit this openly. I don't know what to do to stop these negative feelings of mine. I can see how frustrated my boyfriend is, telling me everyday that he's not doing anything. In fact, it has caused a lot of fights. I can't help it. What if I can sense that he is lying?

I think I need to work on myself first. I have had a lot of failed relationships just because they just got tired of defending themselves. The question is, how? Anyway, have a nice day and keep 'em coming!